Vignette Research

BLOOMSBURY RESEARCH METHODS

Edited by Mark Elliot and Jessica Nina Lester

The Bloomsbury Research Methods series provides authoritative introductions to key and emergent research methods across a range of disciplines.

Each book introduces the key elements of a particular method and/ or methodology and includes examples of its application. Written in an accessible style by leading experts in the field, this series is an innovative pedagogical and research resource.

Also available in the series

Forthcoming in the series

RESEARCH METHODS

Vignette Research

EVI AGOSTINI, MICHAEL SCHRATZ AND IRMA ELOFF

BLOOMSBURY ACADEMIC
LONDON • NEW YORK • OXFORD • NEW DELHI • SYDNEY

BLOOMSBURY ACADEMIC
Bloomsbury Publishing Plc
50 Bedford Square, London, WC1B 3DP, UK
1385 Broadway, New York, NY 10018, USA
29 Earlsfort Terrace, Dublin 2, Ireland

BLOOMSBURY, BLOOMSBURY ACADEMIC and the Diana logo are
trademarks of Bloomsbury Publishing Plc

First published in Great Britain 2024

Series design: Charlotte James
Cover image © shuoshu / iStock

A catalogue record for this book is available from the British Library.

A catalog record for this book is available from the Library of Congress.

ISBN: HB: 978-1-3502-9938-2
       PB: 978-1-3502-9937-5
       ePDF: 978-1-3502-9939-9
       eBook: 978-1-3502-9940-5

Series: Bloomsbury Research Methods

Typeset by RefineCatch Limited, Bungay, Suffolk
Printed and bound in Great Britain

To find out more about our authors and books visit
www.bloomsbury.com and sign up for our newsletters.

*To all who are captivated by life's moments and explore
their beauty from within.*

CONTENTS

FIGURES

TABLES

SERIES EDITORS' FOREWORD

The idea behind this book series is a simple one: to provide concise and accessible introductions to frequently used research methods and to current issues in research methodology. Books in the series have been written by experts in their fields with a brief to write about their subject for a broad audience.

The series has been developed through a partnership between Bloomsbury and the UK's National Centre for Research Methods (NCRM). The original "what is" series sprang from the eponymous strand at NCRM's popular Research Methods Festivals which have run biennially since 2004.

This relaunched series reflects changes in the research landscape, embracing research methods innovation and interdisciplinarity. Methodological innovation is the order of the day, and the books provide updates to the latest developments whilst still maintaining an emphasis on accessibility to a wide audience. The format allows researchers who are new to a field to gain an insight into its key features, while also providing a useful update on recent developments for people who have had some prior acquaintance with it. All readers should find it helpful to be taken through the discussion of key terms, the history of how the method or methodological issue has developed, and the assessment of the strengths and possible weaknesses of the approach through analysis of illustrative examples.

This book is devoted to the innovative and provocative topic of vignette research. In this book the authors – Evi Agostini, Michael Schratz and Irma Eloff – introduce researchers to the foundations of vignette research, as well as the process of deploying and evaluating this methodology. The approach to vignette research that Agostini and colleagues present, which has its origins in phenomenology, is one that they have all been integrally involved in developing. They thus offer a nuanced and personal overview of the history of this approach, which at its core is focused on presenting experiences in a way that minimizes the distance between the researchers and researched.

Notably, Agostini and colleagues make explicit the origins of vignette research, and, in so doing, explicate how its links to phenomenology make it unique from other qualitative approaches to research, such as ethnography. Moreover, throughout the book, Agostini and colleagues emphasize that their approach to vignette research focuses on capturing the experiences of others as they occur in the given research context, while the researcher takes a co-experiential position. To this end, they discuss not just why but how vignette research is not about *describing* an event or experience, but rather *showing* it to the reader.

What makes their book particularly unique is that it offers both the philosophical foundations of the method, as well as a clear pathway for how to *do* and *evaluate* vignette research. As such, readers both familiar with and new to vignette research will find useful insights into both what vignette research is and how to craft a provocative and grounded vignette.

The books in this series aim to equip readers with a broad sense of why a given method deserves to be taken seriously. Indeed, Agostini and colleagues do just this in this book – that is, they illustrate the value of vignette research, and in so doing, make visible its power as a social science research method.

Jessica Nina Lester & Mark Elliot
Series editors

FOREWORD

Why is it that so much social scientific research comes across as strangely bloodless and disconnected from the great questions of our time? Universities around the world turn out doctoral students year after year who command impressive knowledge of quantitative and qualitative methodologies, yet for much of the public, their findings often seem to be trivial or irrelevant. It's not only matters of technical sophistication that can lead many people to keep research at arm's length. When one considers the emotional intensity of life in both the public and private spheres, the distanced, stilted and dissatisfying nature of so much research leaves one suspicious of the whole enterprise, as if all of the drama and pathos has been drained out of the density of everyday experiences and a desiccated husk is all that remains.

If you've ever struggled with similar feelings about the disconnect between the richness of experience and the alienating aspects of so much research, this small jewel of a book is for you. Here, the authors' aspiration is to write vignettes that place 'the authors inside events' (see the section entitled 'Vignette research as a human experience') instead of being objectified and estranged from them. This invites researchers to participate in the multifaceted episodes that make up the many overlapping strata of our lives with their whole selves. Just as billions of people across the globe each day encounter not just one another's intellects, but also their emotions, bodies and imaginations, so researchers should endeavour to get close to these sensations in the quest to understand 'an invisible world of experiences' (see the section entitled 'Vignette research as a human experience') and to render them capable of closer analysis and further transformation.

What kinds of experiences might 'vignette researchers' select for investigation? In vivid descriptions throughout this book, we see people interacting with one another in a myriad of deceptively simple ways that call for closer analysis to unpack their true meaning. We also see researchers who are questioning what they are finding and sharing their writing with their research subjects, thereby promoting the kind of sustained intersubjectivity between insiders and outsiders that can heighten awareness of problems first intuited, and subsequently identified and named in collaboration with vignette researchers. By taking the time to write with meticulous, narrative flair and by combining vignettes with guiding questions, vignette researchers are opening up new venues for investigating just what is happening in our societies and why.

Examples of the kinds of questions raised in this book include: In our quest for ever greater levels of accountability and transparency, are we overlooking the depth and breadth of experiences and forgoing a wealth of opportunities for understanding what is really transpiring and why? In seeking to strengthen the smooth functioning of civil society, are we overlooking opportunities for shared inquiry that might lead to social transformations that could benefit everyone in the long run? In our emphasis upon cognition, are we overlooking the embodied, affective dimensions of human experiences and neglecting to attend to their depth in the process?

These are not trivial questions, but they somehow elude rigorous interrogation in much of mainstream scholarship. The development and pursuit of vignette research, the authors tell us, allows us to explore our assumptions about how society should work, in order to question and probe more deeply than ever before into the nature of our interactions. This requires an initial 'withholding [of] judgement' so that the researcher retains their 'rootedness in the raw data' (see 'Show, don't tell' section) and its superflux of meanings and implications. This 'suspension or bracketing of hasty judgement' (see 'The phenomenological attitude' section) then creates new space for shared dialogue and renewed practice.

It all sounds promising, but one word of warning is warranted for English speakers. Many of the ideas and practices explored in this book emerge from the philosophical tradition of phenomenology and the demands it places upon all of those who want to get up close to practice, with no pretence of elucidating generalizable principles from the superflux of experience. This tradition is linguistically multilayered, drawing upon classical Greek and Latin sources combined with twentieth-century continental philosophical forays that are likely to be unfamiliar to many readers. Stick with the text, however, and soon enough its intellectual demands will become energizing and uplifting. The analysis can and should be read over and over again. Persevere, and you'll find that the descriptions of vignette research yield new possibilities and pleasures with each reading, which open up a plethora of promising ways of understanding social life in its textured, dynamic complexity.

Dennis Shirley, Boston College, USA

ACKNOWLEDGEMENTS

We would like to thank the many colleagues, vignette research groups, students and anonymous reviewers who contributed in different ways to this book; some provided detailed and invaluable comments on an earlier draft and some contributed their own work. Our particular thanks go to Johanna F. Schwarz, a founding member of Innsbruck Vignette Research (IVR), for her experience report, and to our vignette writers Markus Ammann, Theresa Hauck, Bernhard Nairz, Tamara Peer, Hans Karl Peterlini, Anna Pritz, Johanna F. Schwarz, Tanja Westfall-Greiter and Megan Swart.

We would like to thank the three institutions whose faculties/centres we were members of during the period in which the book was written – the University of Vienna, the University of Innsbruck and the University of Pretoria – for their academic, administrative, technical, collegial and financial support.

We would also like to thank Fatima-Sahra Al-Khatib for her help during the final phase of completing this book.

We also owe thanks to Sarah Rimmington and Sharon Ball, whose meticulous and exacting translation work opened the door to greater empathy, appreciation and resonance.

Our deep appreciation to researchers and scholars around the world who are embracing vignette research, co-developing this ever-evolving methodology and sharing their wisdom in ways that enrich and deepen our understanding of life and the world we live in.

Vignette Research **was published with the support of the Austrian Science Fund (FWF): PUB 1023-P.**

ABBREVIATIONS

IVR   Innsbruck Vignette Research
PLC   Professional Learning Community
SDGs Sustainable Development Goals

Introduction

Dear Reader,

Welcome to our book, which invites you on a journey of exploration into a unique research approach and new ways of involving the researcher and the researched. This journey began in Austria, at the heart of Europe, and has since stopped at many destinations on different continents. Its starting point was the University of Innsbruck, where a research team was awarded a research grant allowing them to explore the nature of student learning.[1] Learning is based on very personal experiences and makes people who they are, and at the time, the research team was unable to find a suitable research method in either the quantitative or the qualitative research camp.

As the team searched, they came across the quote 'Meanings only inspired by remote, confused, inauthentic intuitions – if by any intuitions at all – are not enough: we must go back "to the things themselves"' (Quoted in Moran 2008: 22). This goes back to Edmund Husserl in the years 1900/1901, who introduced phenomenology as a philosophical method. Subsequently, different schools of phenomenology have developed, and have taken many different directions. For those authors among us who have joined this movement, Husserl's call to go 'back "to the things themselves"' (ibid.) became a waymarker for the development of a descriptive, phenomenologically oriented approach, which has now taken a firm foothold in the research landscape in the form of vignette research: the study of lived experience.

This volume aims to explore the rich legacy of empirical thinking in an original, innovative, phenomenological exploration of experience as it reveals itself 'as something' to the context in which the researcher is interested. The primary target audience is scholars and researchers in the field of vignette research. We have designed this book as a travel guide; on the one hand to lead you into some unexpected terrain within the research landscape, and on the other hand to provide you with empirically verified steps to enable you to deploy vignette research yourself. The usefulness of vignette research has been proven across a variety of disciplines and professions with an interest in experience, because lived experience is terrain that affects us all.

Since this approach has now aroused widespread interest beyond the German-speaking world, we are responding to the wish expressed by many for an English-language introduction to vignette research, and have compiled a 'best of' list with regard to a variety of fields. The personal gains from any journey depend not least on the expectations you bring to it and the way you prepare for it. So we want to prepare you to encounter some potential irritations, as vignette research is in some respects radically different from traditional approaches.

A first irritation is probably that the descriptive phenomenological approach to the perception of an experience used here does not build on the knowledge we already have, but rather sees such knowledge as an obstacle to advancing 'to the things themselves' (ibid.). Vignette researchers must first 'bracket' their assumptions, presumptions or hypotheses, i.e., hold back, in order to grasp what is revealed in as unbiased a manner as possible. It is only this exploratory openness that makes it possible for the phenomenologically oriented approach to perceive the unknown in the known. In this context, it is essential to extend perception to include all the senses, since this will determine what we experience, and how we experience it 'as something', and offer new insights.

The second irritation lies in the fact that vignette research does not attempt to deliver universally valid insights, but rather explores the particular contained within the general. Since situational experiences are unique in their respective contexts, they cannot be generalized – just as, conversely, individuals cannot be found in statistical data. Hence, vignettes bring out the particularity or singularity of a certain phenomenon or event while at the same time providing access to a more general or universal meaning. Objectivity, reliability and validity are not appropriate criteria for determining their quality. The power of a vignette lies in the conciseness (*Prägnanz*) with which it describes the multiplicity that characterizes a lifeworld experience, and that generates resonance in the reader.

A third irritation may result from the need to take the subjectivity of the researcher seriously. While researchers deploying conventional approaches enter the research field in as distanced a manner as possible – the objective observer being the outsider who attempts to focus in detail on what is happening without becoming directly involved – vignette researchers seek the greatest possible proximity in order to experience the experience of others in a situation 'up close'; namely, corporeally (*leiblich*). In this experience, the researcher is not only a witness to what is revealed, but this experience does something to him or her: it has a transformational effect. The process of creating a vignette allows for it to be based on the phenomena that are co-experientially made manifest.

One further irritation, as you may already have realized, is that the concepts and contexts of phenomenology are unfamiliar and take some getting used to. Phenomenology is characterized by the expressive spirit of the time in which it emerged, which in many cases goes back to Greek and Latin roots. Husserl, the German founding father of phenomenology, built his philosophy of thought on the scientific traditions of Greek philosophical history, and this is reflected in his terminology. In order to make this connection comprehensible, in some cases we have appended the original German expression to the English translation in brackets (this also gives you the opportunity to trace the meanings and etymology of the terms for yourself).

If you are wondering why vignette research takes such an idiosyncratic and methodologically unusual path, the answer is that the academic approach and underlying theory of phenomenology is based on the study of appearances, the study of the phenomenon as a given, in contrast to the logos that prevails in more usual research discourse. This unfamiliar approach is also manifest in the expressive style of the vignette, which is at the heart of vignette research. To this end, we start our research journey by presenting a vignette crafted by Irma Eloff in South Africa on the basis of an online conversation with Evi Agostini and Michael Schratz in Austria, which took place after the completion of the manuscript and in which the three authors discussed their impressions.[2]

Vignette 1: 'Editors' meeting'

It is the day of the solstice. Midsummer in Europe. The longest day and the shortest night. 'I am curious about the outcome of this,' Professor Prinz says, laughing. Behind him on the screen, there are rows of books at different heights and a picture of a green plant against a dark background. Joining him online, Professor Moretti sits wearing earphones. An office cabinet behind her seems to create a frame around her. There is a noticeboard covered with little notes and cards on the side wall of her office. They discuss the ways in which a book on vignette research can be brought to a close. 'When you write, a lot of things come into your mind . . . you know what I mean?' she asks inquisitively. 'We have been doing it for such a long time,' she states matter-of-factly. 'You have to be fair, and more precise,' he confirms. She smiles. He looks to the left, staring into the distance. 'We had to move from a German approach to an Anglo-American approach,' he proclaims with a concerned look, 'transposing the material into another culture.' 'Yes', she adds with her eyebrows slightly raised, 'while not writing in your mother tongue.' The discussion turns to the most challenging aspects of writing the book. 'Immersing myself in the philosophical world and then at the same time being very pragmatic,' he ventures. She nods, twirling a frond of her hair and playing softly with it between her fingers. 'Being more scientific, or more advisory . . . ?' she reflects. 'You have to ask, where would a novice start – the practical part,' he asserts, looking to the left again. 'It's a balancing act,' he declares, 'and it is for the readers, too'.

> Vignette writer: Irma Eloff, 23 June 2022, editors' meeting, Pretoria, South Africa, unpublished.

The balancing act at the end of this vignette refers to the successful dovetailing of an orderly, academically given, pre-articulated concept and a situated, co-experiential experience, weaving them together into a texture of lived experience. You will learn more about this at several points on your journey through this volume. However, at this stage, we do not want to hide the fact that the three of us had to laugh heartily after our co-experiential experience in the creation of this vignette. To that end, we share with you a quote from Umberto Eco's introduction to academic work (1988: 265): 'Writing a piece of research means having fun, and doing the work is like slaughtering a pig, as the Italians say: "You don't throw anything away."[3] We recommend that you take Eco's advice on board!

You may be irritated by the design of vignettes: as a narrative text type, they are unusual in the research context. When we first started using this novel approach, we had to get used to this too. Vignette research is a new type of knowledge production and necessitates a new relationship between researchers and researched. It disrupts the view that theory and practice can be kept separate; and, when we make use of all the affective spheres of the lifeworld we live in, the commitment to and practice of research are as much personal as they are scholarly. Although vignettes seem loosely written, skills are required to craft them.

Bruno Latour, a well-known researcher on scientific research, teaches us that serious research requires one to be able to change one's mode of expression and style, if only out of respect for the specifics of the subject matter in question. For him, 'changing your style is a way of showing respect for the topic in question, and making sure you do not transpose the same issues from one topic to another' (Latour 1997: 43). It is helpful to keep this quote in mind when you start crafting your first vignettes. As is the case elsewhere, practice makes perfect.

Now that you have faced the aforementioned irritations with regard to your expectations, you will be prepared for your journey into the research world described in this book. Confrontation with the unfamiliar is an integral feature of a phenomenological approach and gives rise to the appropriate attitude. We have done as much as we can to prepare you for the journey. However, be aware when using this book as a travel guide: the map is not the terrain!

Evi Agostini, Michael Schratz and Irma Eloff

PART ONE

Understanding Vignette Research

CHAPTER ONE

What is Vignette Research?

In order to understand the scientific background to vignette research, some clarification is necessary. To this end, the term 'vignette' must first be set against the phenomenological background. This chapter introduces you to the philosophical foundation of vignette research, which requires a particular approach. The researcher needs to capture the phenomena that reveal themselves in a form that gives the reader of the data the feeling of being there in the scene. In vignette research, therefore, data are generated by the researcher *within* the experience itself, rather than being obtained *from* the experience. The chapter explains this embodied interrelationship, which has transformative power: it does something to and with the researcher. This makes vignette research unique among qualitative approaches. It concludes with a synopsis comparing vignette research with other empirical approaches to field research, highlighting the nuanced differences between them.

Vignettes in and out of research

The word 'vignette' has many meanings. If you search for it on Wikipedia, you will find more than ten entries, from contexts ranging from philately to literature to music to sports, illustrating the colourful history of the term and its meaning. The word 'vignette' itself goes back to the French word *vignette* (small vine) and was used to describe decorative leaves in illustrations or photographic prints. In psychological, sociological or philosophical experiments, and in the context of assessment centres and surveys, a vignette refers to a hypothetical initial situation that aims to prompt someone to arrive at personal judgements or (normative) conclusions and beliefs (see, for example, Finch 1987).[4] Depending on the research context, interview situation, laboratory experiment or test structure (e.g. dilemmas, moral judgements), this enables responses to be assessed or classified – in a mostly predefined and personality-related way.

If you are looking for a more authoritative source for vignettes, Frederick Erickson's chapter on qualitative methods in research on teaching in the third edition of the American Educational Research Association's *Handbook of Research on Teaching* is a good resource. Erickson (1986: 150) refers to the Greek tradition of rhetoric, where orators were recommended to use 'richly descriptive vignettes in their speeches to persuade the audience that the orator's general assertions were true in particular cases'.[5] Building on this historical tradition, he lists analytic narrative vignettes as one of nine main elements of a report on fieldwork research, defining them as follows:

> The narrative vignette is a vivid portrayal of the conduct of an event of everyday life, in which the sights and sounds of what was being said and done are described in the natural sequence of their occurrence in real time. The moment-to-moment style of description in a narrative vignette gives the reader a sense of being there in the scene.
>
> ERICKSON 1986: 150

This quote already highlights significant features of relevance to vignette research. As a 'vivid portrayal' (ibid.) of an event in daily life, the vignette records what is happening at the moment of the researcher's presence. The intention is to record not only the course of action, but also multi-sensory perceptions, as underlined by 'sight and sound' (ibid.). While an objective, distanced scientific text conveys abstract findings from the empirical work, the vignette condenses what is experienced in the field into a narrative that is as true to the experience as possible, to give the reader 'a sense of being there in the scene' (ibid.). An important function of the vignette is to allow the reader to relive the events recorded by the researcher as closely as possible, rather than to reconstruct them. To do so, the researcher emphasizes aspects he or she considers important, while others are relegated to the background or omitted. Therefore, in vignette writing 'some details are sketched in and others are left out; some features are sharpened and heightened in their portrayal . . . and other features are softened, or left to merge with the background' (ibid.).

Referring to Erickson's chapter, Charalambos Vrasidas (2001: 99) defines the vignette as a 'vivid description of the setting that communicates how life in the setting actually is'. He reports how vignettes helped to clarify his thoughts and arguments when reflecting on distance education:

> The vignette's validity should be determined by the degree to which it is rich in description and includes enough interpretive perspective. The vignette and the rich descriptions of concrete details and procedures allow the reader to be coanalyst of the study. The report should have enough evidence that will allow the reader to make her own judgements about the plausibility of my account. . . . The vignettes allowed me to present a 'slice of life' from the setting in a way that illustrates the key characteristics of each situation.
>
> VRASIDAS 2001: 99

For Vrasidas, in order to capture a 'slice of life' (ibid.), the researcher positions him or herself on the continuum between observer and participant. Therefore, the closeness to or distance from the participants in the setting influences the kind of data collection the researcher is able to undertake. Vrasidas also points out another significant aspect for vignette research: researchers face the challenge of articulating in words not only the visible but also the audible and the sensory. They strive to clarify and highlight the impossible plurality and excesses of life (Schratz, Schwarz and Westfall-Greiter 2013). According to Bernhard Waldenfels (2002: 138), an important German phenomenological philosopher, there is always a surplus in what we see, hear and feel, the richness of which cannot be fully articulated. Therefore, the researcher can only capture the full extent of the aforementioned 'slice of life' (Vrasidas 2001: 99) by attending to all their senses. Moreover, researchers are confronted with the need to express such richness adequately in the research data. Vignettes make this possible by acting as a vessel, mirroring experience as closely as possible.

These early insights into the use of vignettes in both quantitative and qualitative social research highlight important features of vignette research, but stem from the interpretative tradition. In this understanding, the researcher's intention is to analyse and interpret the acquisition of knowledge in a particular way. Thus, Erickson (1986: 150) sees two tasks for the narrator in writing the vignette: the first is educational ('the narrator must ground the more abstract analytical concepts of the study in concrete particulars'), and the second is rhetorical:

> by providing adequate evidence that the author has made a valid analysis of what the happenings meant from the point of view of the actors in the event. The particular description contained in the analytic narrative vignette both explains to the reader the author's analytic constructs by instantiation and convinces the reader that such an event could and did happen that way.
>
> ERICKSON 1986: 150

The prefix 'analytic' (ibid.) indicates that the vignette author is concerned with presenting an abstract fact in a comprehensible manner, going beyond mere graphs and frequency of occurrence tables. For Erickson it is the task of the researcher 'to persuade the reader that the event described was typical, that is, that one can generalize from this instance to other analogous instances in the author's data corpus' (ibid.).

In this volume in the Research Methods series we take a different, even opposite, approach to the use of vignettes. The approach in this book has its origins in descriptive phenomenology, a philosophy which 'does not expect to arrive at an understanding of man and the world from any starting point other than that of their "facticity" ... It is a matter of describing, not of explaining or analysing' (Merleau-Ponty 2009: vii/ix). Consequently, the purpose of the vignette here is not to explain or reconstruct what happened but rather to recreate the experience. This understanding accentuates some of the fundamentals of descriptive phenomenology, and we discuss these in the 'Accessing the lifeworld from within' section.

Accessing the lifeworld from within

Vignette research uses phenomenological ways of thinking and perceiving to explore the lived experience of everyday situations. It attempts to make difficult-to-record phenomena in everyday life and work accessible to scientific observation through methods other than empirical research, which tries to abstract generalizable data from the living world. Robin Whittemore, Susan K. Chase and Carol Lynn Mandle (2001: 522) refer to the challenges of building validity standards into qualitative research 'because of the necessity to incorporate rigour and subjectivity as well as creativity in the scientific process'. Discussing validity in different qualitative approaches, they point out that phenomenological inquiry must attend in particular to explicitness, vividness and thoroughness (Whittemore, Chase and Mandle 2001).

In order to take these validity criteria into account, it is necessary to get as close as possible to the action. To explore the learning experiences in school in the original Innsbruck Vignette Research (IVR) group, it was necessary to obtain experiential data on students in the classroom. Given that the researcher can never completely experience the experience of others, it is clear that no methodology can fully achieve this goal. As a consequence, it was necessary for them to be as close as possible to the experience and to make the experienced conscious. For Max Van Manen (1990: 9), consciousness

is the only access human beings have to the world. Or rather, it is by virtue of being conscious that we are already related to the world. Thus, all we can ever know must present itself to consciousness. Whatever falls outside of consciousness, therefore, falls outside the bounds of our possible lived experience. Consciousness is always transitive. To be conscious is to be aware, in some sense, of some aspect of the world. And thus phenomenology is keenly interested in the significant world of the human being.

In order to raise awareness of the researcher's relationship with people and things in the field, it was essential for the IVR group to develop methods for co-experiencing and protocolling lived experiences in light of the goals of their study. The researchers recorded their co-experiential experience of the situation in writing *in statu nascendi* [Latin for 'in the state of being born', 'just as something is about to begin']. They noted what was immediately apprehended by the senses before making any final judgement and subsequently condensed these notes into a concise narrative text that recorded the co-experiential experience. The resulting vignettes took the form of a 'dense description' (Geertz 1991) or 'condensed description' (Gabriel 2010) of the primary experiences recorded in the field. As an experience-based text type, the vignette depicts an everyday event as closely as possible to the lived experience. Its essence is the experiential moments by which researchers are affected in the field (e.g. at school, at home, in hospital, in traffic, outdoors). As a result, the vignette comprises short, concise narratives in which something surprising, special or peculiar is revealed. The conciseness and the *pathic* content [from the Latin or Greek meaning 'suffering', 'passion'] of the condensed narrative should prompt a corresponding response in the vignette reader.

David Geelan (2006: 99) proposes that the validity of phenomenological texts can be seen in their ability to provoke a bodily, emotional response in their readers, who are then inspired to reflect on their own practice. Vignettes put 'someone on a track' (Buck 1989: 145) by going beyond the situation they are targeting. This pathic effect is created not least by taking into account the aforementioned validity criteria of vividness and thoroughness when vignettes are being written (for research criteria, see the 'Quality criteria in qualitative research' section). Vignette texts are therefore not arbitrarily interchangeable, but rather

> like a quotation, the vignette is meant to substantiate statements and thus respond to truth claims as well as convince the reader of them. Not only is the vignette a nuanced description of a scene, but its selection, presentation, and mode of depiction reveal the researcher's reading. The vignette highlights things deemed important to the study, while others are relegated to the background or omitted.
>
> MEYER-DRAWE 2012a: 13

As qualitative research instruments, phenomenological vignettes capture moments of experience from everyday life or from lifeworlds and social spaces, and condense them into brief scenes, which can serve as an example of how something can be seen as situated in time. 'The understanding of examples is here a way of knowing through which one comes to grasp oneself reflexively as one grasped in linguistic accomplishment' (Buck 1981: 105). Here, examples do not refer to an independent generalization but to further examples, whose common features give rise to a family resemblance. However, where does this approach lead? To answer this question, it is necessary to follow the phenomenological trail.

Getting 'to the things themselves'

The basis of vignette research lies in the tradition of phenomenology, which 'is commonly understood in either of two ways: as a disciplinary field in philosophy, or as a movement in the history of philosophy' (Smith 2018). The groundbreaking work of Edmund Husserl, Edith Stein, Martin Heidegger, Hannah Arendt, Emmanuel Lévinas, Maurice Merleau-Ponty, Hans-Georg Gadamer and many others, including Simone de Beauvoir and Jean-Paul Sartre, launched a philosophical movement and thus influenced and perpetuated various cultures. Moreover, phenomenology has become a source of inspiration for research and practice in various disciplines outside of philosophy, such as anthropology, sociology, psychology, psychiatry, medicine, education and architecture.

The phenomenological research of different disciplines is unified by a deep concern about the way the world appears to human beings who experience it. Husserl's call, 'Back to the things themselves!' (2001: 168), which focuses on the way the world appears to the person experiencing it, has inspired many scholars to follow his call and build their work on this philosophical foundation. 'This interest in phenomenology can perhaps be understood in the context of its potential contribution to re-thinking our understanding of the complex phenomena we encounter in the dynamic and, at times, confronting world in which we find ourselves in this 21st century' (Dall'Alba 2009: 1).

In this book we will present vignette research as one of the ways of getting 'to the things themselves' (Husserl 2001: 168). To provide an idea of what a vignette could look like in the context of our approach, we present one that has its origins in school, and which readers from different disciplinary backgrounds may be able to relate to.

Vignette 2: 'Roland meets Mickey Mouse'

> It is silent reading time in the fifth lesson. Everyone knows what to do. Roland turns around and takes a Mickey Mouse comic book from the shelf on the wall behind him. He doesn't even have to stand up from his solitary position in the back row. He lays the booklet on his lap, leans his left arm on the bench, rests his forehead in his hand and immerses himself in reading. Occasionally he laughs at certain parts and says, 'Great!' He flips back and forth several times. In the meantime the teacher talks with groups of students and individuals about organisational matters. After some fifteen minutes, she announces loudly, 'Put all the books away and take out your notebooks!' All the students but Roland follow her instructions. He seems to be lost in his reading, showing no sign of response. The teacher approaches him, asks if he knows what she said. He answers promptly with nonchalance: 'Put all the books away and take out your notebooks!' With a wrinkled nose, he slowly closes the Mickey Mouse comic book.
>
> SCHRATZ, SCHWARZ and
> WESTFALL-GREITER 2012: 64–5

The starting point of phenomenological perception is a human being's experience of the world. Experience builds on the present encounter in which we enter into a relationship with people, things and the world as a whole. In Vignette 2 we learn about Roland, a student sitting in the back row of the classroom who is attracted by a comic book that he seems to be drawn into. The writer of the vignette tries to depict Roland's movements as accurately as possible and, as such, offers the reader a detailed account of the situation. Note that the vignette writer often refers to body movements such as 'turns around', 'takes . . . from the shelf', 'stands up', 'lays on his lap', 'leans . . . on the bench', 'rests in his hand'. This indicates that experience builds on our encounter with the world we are embedded in when we relate to people and things. For body phenomenologists, the body is the medium for this embeddedness in, and engagement with, our world. 'It is because I delve into the thickness of the world by perceptual experience,' says the French body phenomenologist Merleau-Ponty (2009: 237), characterizing the corporeality of lived experience. Waldenfels regards the human body as an original script (*Urskript*) that archives lived experience.

He understands the body as an instrument resonating with experience that in old age can be read as a map of life (Waldenfels 1999).

In Husserl's philosophical approach, the world opens up by showing itself to somebody 'as something'. That which reveals itself to the rescarcher exploring the lifeworld 'as something' is known as a phenomenon (φαινόμενον [phainómenon]; in English: 'appearance', 'impression'). In the original Greek, the term 'phenomenon' means on the one hand that which is revealed, that which shows itself, and on the other hand that which appears. In phenomenology, however, phenomena are not phenomenal in the sense of spectacular, as:

[e]ven the everyday experience of simple objects can serve as the point of departure for a phenomenological analysis. Indeed, if philosophy is to avoid the dead end of stale abstractions, it has to reconnect to the richness of everyday life. Importantly, however, phenomenology is primarily interested in the *how* rather than in the *what* of objects. Rather than focusing on, say, the weight, rarity, or chemical composition of the object, phenomenology is concerned with the way in which the object shows or displays itself, i.e., in how it appears. There are important differences between the ways in which a physical object, a utensil, a work of art, a melody, a state of affairs, a number, or another human being presents itself.

ZAHAVI 2019: 9–10

The appearance of something can show itself in very different ways, depending on which mode of access is chosen, and it always 'begins with experience and remains in experience' (Husserl 1990: 98). However, whichever access mode is chosen, one never sees the whole world, but only a part of it, closely connected to the lived experience of a situation, an issue, an event or a particular practice. In Vignette 2, the researcher's co-experiential experience of Roland's activities with the comic book show themselves to him/her as an immersion in reading ('seems to be lost in his reading'). He or she, however, cannot see more than Roland's actions with the book as giving the impression that he is not following the teacher's instructions.

Phenomenology, in this sense, is the attempt to perceive the appearances of things, contexts or situations in their diversity and ambiguity and to describe their appearance (something-as-something) from the point of view of the respective mode of experience. For Merleau-Ponty (2009: 196), 'ambiguity is the essence of human existence, and everything we live or think has always several meanings'. The reader of Vignette 2 is left with this ambiguity when reading Roland's echoing of the teacher's command while slowly closing the comic book. This is also indicated by the researcher's reference to the bodily perception of the wrinkled nose. In this way, vignettes are open to multiple readers and to multiple readings. This self-contextualization of the experience obstructs any one definitive interpretation or conclusion, so that the reader is compelled to engage again and again in dialogue with what is there.

Accessing the fragility of human action

In the multitude of traditions and receptions of Husserlian phenomenology since the 1920s, most approaches take for granted that one universal structure of experience is its intentionality: a human being's attention is always directed to something and never innocent or neutral. How he or she perceives what occurs in the field, be it observing, analysing, acting, remembering or co-experiencing, has a strong influence on how the emerging meaning is attributed (Schwarz 2018: 112).

Schratz et al. (2022) use the following example to illustrate this intentionality of attention through different modalities of experience: The apple tree in front of the house exists even if we do not look at it. If people look at it, it shows itself to them 'as something' in different ways. Perhaps it is in full bloom and delights the heart. Or its leaves are falling, reminding us that summer will soon be over. A hiker passing by encounters the tree as a provider of shade, and a biologist would be attracted by the biodiversity of the creatures living in the tree. So, the tree shows itself in different manifestations and, depending on the observer and his or her attention, 'as something' completely different. Nevertheless, it is always the same tree, even if one can never grasp it in its completeness. Therefore, one can grasp the tree only partially – at least not simultaneously from the front and the back, from above and below, from inside and outside. Moreover, memories of earlier perceptions always interfere with the present perception. Therefore, perceptions are a constant mixture of familiarity and unfamiliarity. This is true not only for objects such as a tree, but also for the social world (Rumpf 2010: 23–4). Phenomenology is built on unavailability and fragility, which shows up as ambiguities in human actions.

Applying the phenomenological understanding of intentionality to the lifeworld of organizations, Wendelin Küpers (2015) points to the inseparable relatedness and connectedness of organization members to phenomena in their lifeworld and in its interwoven practices:

> All their individual perceiving, remembering, imagining, planning, acting, etc. are always related to something or someone as they appear in organizational everyday life. Intentional orientations shape not only how organizational members inhabit their workspace/place, but also how they approach and apprehend (or not) this world, especially as one of a shared inhabitancy. Even more, intentionality of practitioners discloses 'who' or 'what' they direct (or not) their attentions, energies and actions towards.
>
> KÜPERS 2015: 127–8

The phenomenological approach does not look for causal relations between what happens between people in social settings but rather asks how 'something-as-something' shows itself to someone exploring the lifeworld (*In-der-Welt-sein*) in a social setting (e.g. organization). Therefore, phenomenologists 'distinguish between a thing and its appearances, a distinction that Heidegger has called the "ontological difference", the difference between a thing and the presencing (or absencing) of the thing' (Sokolowski 2000: 50). However, we do not have access to reality, and that is why 'something shows itself as something' only in the experience itself, which has a present meaning for the person concerned (in the given example the observer, hiker, biologist . . .) and encounters it 'as something' in that particular situation. German sociologist Hartmut Rosa (2018: 8) speaks of a 'resonance relationship' as an 'interplay between that which is available to us and that which remains unavailable to us, but which nevertheless "concerns" us'.

But what does this have to do with our vignette research? To answer this question, we must refer back to Vignette 2 ('Roland meets Mickey Mouse'). In the classroom scene, the researcher's attention is attracted by Roland's engagement with the comic book. In co-experiencing this lesson, the researcher cannot see or describe everything that is happening but relates to what resonates with them in the experiential flow of the action. Within this resonance experienced by the researcher lies what Rosa calls this interplay between what is available and what remains unavailable but nevertheless concerns him or her. There might be a multitude of meanings in the situation, but they are excluded when a vignette is composed. Interpretations would lead away from the 'things themselves' (Husserl 2001: 168). Max Van Manen (1990: 9) has explored lived experience as 'human science for an action sensitive pedagogy' in his work and explains the scientific positioning of the phenomenological approach:

> Phenomenology aims to gain a deeper understanding of the nature or meaning of our everyday experiences. Phenomenology asks, 'What is this or that kind of experience like?' It differs from almost every other science in that it attempts to gain insightful descriptions of the way we experience the world pre-reflectively, without taxonomizing, classifying, or abstracting it. So phenomenology does not offer us the possibility of effective theory with which we can now explain and/or control the world, but rather it offers us the possibility of plausible insights that bring us into more direct contact with the world.
>
>   VAN MANEN 1990: 9

As a phenomenological approach, vignette research is exploratory in nature, attempting to access the experiential base of knowledge in, and through exploration of, lifeworlds in everyday settings. The researcher must enter into the experiential worlds he or she wants to explore through research. Therefore, our approach involves sharing lived experiences in the field (e.g. school, workplace, hospital, museum, traffic and so on). The vignette methodology enables researchers to capture the experience of others' experience as it occurs in the field, where researchers adopt a stance we refer to as 'co-experiential experience'. Contact with the lifeworld is about the resonance of lived experience in the field, which shows itself in the researcher in co-experiencing 'as something'. This co-experiential experience refers to 'the attempt to understand the experiences of the world, the other and of myself, even if there is an inevitable distance between my concrete, situated experiences and my return to them while I am talking or thinking about them' (Meyer-Drawe 2017: 14).

In co-experiential experience, the researcher's attitude plays an important role: the attention of the research is not directed towards the expected behaviour of people in the field, for instance the observance of rules in road traffic or the cognitive activation of students by teachers in school lessons. Rather, the attention of the research is directed towards something that shows itself 'as something' (the original meaning of 'phenomenon'). This is where the validity criterion of explicitness, or 'investigator bias', comes into play.[6] In his phenomenological work, Husserl (1962) coined the Greek term *epoché*, referring to a kind of bracketing (see Box 1).

Box 1 Epoché

Epoché (ἐποχή [epokhē]), the ancient Greek term, is typically translated as 'suspension', meaning 'suspension of judgement' and 'withholding of assent'. It was introduced by Edmund Husserl as a means of distancing oneself from one's prejudices, a phenomenological reduction that 'brackets' theories, conclusions, and hypotheses in order to arrive at insights into the 'essence' of the thing.

In phenomenological research, *epoché*, or bracketing, is a process of precluding biases and assumptions to explain a phenomenon in terms of its own inherent system of meaning. It is a general attitude one must assume before commencing phenomenological study and involves taking systematic steps to 'set aside' assumptions and beliefs about a phenomenon to examine how it presents itself in the participant's world. Bracketing is therefore not non-judgement, but postponement of judgement.

The first step is to bracket the validity of the world and thus the pre-judgement of an implicitly presupposed transcendence of the natural world by means of *epoché*. This specifically philosophical attitude, which is accompanied by a suspension of any naive metaphysical attitude (Husserl 1962: 260) and is described by Husserl (1962: 154) as the precondition for reduction, leads to the second step, reduction, or engagement with the connection between subjectivity and the world (Husserl 1973: 61). Phenomenological reduction thus requires researchers to reflect sceptically on the relationship between the object of perception and its perceivers, and what shows itself (*noema*) is traced back to the way it shows itself (*noesis*) (Waldenfels 1992): the what leads them back to the how. Malte Brinkmann (2018) distinguishes between three models of *epoché*, referring to different phenomenologists.

Source: Authors

Bracketing is central to descriptive phenomenological analysis; as Waldenfels (1992: 30) recommends, researchers should honour the uniqueness of their own and others' experience while consciously ignoring it as they attempt to extrapolate 'what reveals itself, through how it reveals itself'. The unbiased openness to the perception of what attracts the researcher requires us to bracket pre-existing theoretical concepts so that these are not applied to the research genre from the outset. Such an attitude 'requires a certain distance, a special form of ethnological *epoché*, to bring the unfamiliar as unfamiliar into view and to help the unfamiliar as unfamiliar to express itself' (Waldenfels 2007: 47). This addresses the basic focus that should help researchers to arrive at the 'things themselves' (Husserl 2001: 168).

The unavailability of everyday life/ embodied subjectivity

Before we elaborate on the verbal texture of the vignette obtained through the co-experiential experience of lived experience in the research field, the question remains: Which moments *in statu nascendi* of lived experience does the researcher select from the stream of experience to create a vignette? By what will he or she be affected? However, this question cannot be answered, since experiences are not predictable or repeatable, and they can only occur once in the temporal and spatial context in question. Therefore, the moment of being affected by the experience of people and things cannot be predicted, but neither can it be forced or impeded (Rosa 2018: 44). Vignettes relate to moments of experience that affect researchers in the field through the immediate corporeal apprehension of the senses before any judgement is made.

Phenomenologists speak of consciousness prior to reflection. They claim 'that an explicit reflective self-consciousness is possible only because there is an ongoing pre-reflective self-awareness built into experience' (Gallagher 2012: 127). Referring to Merleau-Ponty's work, Luis Aguiar de Sousa (2019) elaborates on the sphere of consciousness prior to reflection:

> Not only does this pre-reflective sphere precede and make reflection possible, but it is in this sphere, before any other, that it is possible to find not only my original relation to the world but also my relation or openness towards others. 'Pre-reflective' or 'phenomenological' subjectivity is not absolute. It encompasses the world as much as the world encompasses it; it is a bodily perspective on a world in which it at the same time inheres or is rooted.
>
> AGUIAR de SOUSA 2019: 52

This pre-reflective self-awareness means that our attention is already directed towards somebody or something before we consciously reflect on an experience and react to it. For Merleau-Ponty (2009: 239), the body is 'the subject of perception', because we perceive the world with our body. Therefore, vignette research asks for holistic involvement on the part of the researcher, who should adopt a kind of seismographic attitude, in order to be open to '[t]he fine sense of something that is questionable and uncertain' (Dewey 1995: 75, cited in Rumpf 2010: 28). When we are touched by an experience, the event itself is not particularly significant, but is capable of assuming great meaning (Arrighetti 2007: 79–81). These are experiences that claim us, thwart our expectations, call us to wonder and provoke amazement.

Vignettes 3–5 show how different everyday experiences in public spaces (Vignette 3 and Vignette 4) and institutional contexts (Vignette 5) holistically caught researchers' attention, appealing to them as something worth writing about from their co-experiential experience.

Vignette 3: 'On the pavement'

> A young woman is striding along the pavement, throwing her arms alternately back and forth, her head moving slightly back and forth, and briefly craning her neck. On the cycle lane immediately to the left, a cyclist comes towards her, his gaze fixed on the woman coming towards him. Almost imperceptibly, her step becomes stiffer, she turns her head slightly to the right; the swinging of her head to either side that accompanies the walking step freezes. The cyclist's gaze remains fixed on the woman for a moment, then, as they pass by each other, he turns his head to the other side.

> PETERLINI 2020: 29

Vignette 4: 'The principal on tour with her students'

> 'That's the university,' says Ms. Buch, pointing at the old, elongated building with her right hand. Michael, Thomas, Rudi and Dominique are gathered in a semicircle around the principal of the hospital school, who is taking them on a walk through the city. Ms. Buch is also the head of the learning group for the students who have recently been admitted to the stammering clinic as inpatients. For five weeks, the four children will be undergoing inpatient stammering therapy in the afternoons and attending lessons at the hospital school in the mornings. It may be their last hope of being able to speak without anxiety. On this cold early winter morning, their hands are in their jackets, and their gazes are serious. Only Dominique is smiling, slightly embarrassed. 'And in the summer, the students like to sit on this big lawn here in front of the university and enjoy the sunshine,' Ms. Buch suddenly says. 'And if you go on to study in the city too, perhaps one day you'll be sitting on this lawn as well,' she continues in an enthusiastic tone of voice. Her eyes are sparkling. When Michael, Thomas, Rudi and Dominique hear her words, they flick their heads to the side. Their eyes widen a little, and they exchange glances, nodding self-confidently.

> AMMANN 2018: 6

Vignette 5: 'Listening and reading in English class'

In the English lesson, the students are listening to a dialogue on the CD and reading along in their textbooks. Swaying his torso, Chris glances back and forth between the text in his book, the class, and the teacher. Cora follows the lines of text slowly with her index finger. *Jessica: Can you play the guitar? Pete: Yes, I can.* A loud, dissonant sound follows Pete's answer. Chris' body tenses, a smile appears on his face. He checks quickly in his book, then looks up and scans the class. His eyes return to the dialogue and search the text back and forth, up and down. His smile remains. As Cora hears the dissonant guitar playing, she hesitates briefly, moves her index finger back to the beginning of the line, and slightly raises the corners of her mouth. She raises her head and removes her finger from the text. The CD goes on. She shoves her hands slowly under her thighs. Smiling, she looks out of the window. 'What is this text about?' asks the teacher at the end of the listening task. Chris' hand shoots up, he is glowing. Cora raises her right hand slowly and moves her torso hesitatingly towards the teacher. 'I want to read Pete,' declares Chris in a clear voice. 'That wasn't the question,' says the teacher softly, and waits. Chris smiles silently. The teacher waits and turns to Cora. Her hand is still up in the air, Chris repeats with determination, 'I want to read Pete!' There is no visible reaction. His smile disappears. 'About the perfect job,' Cora answers confidently. The teacher nods and exaggerates her approval by over-articulating. 'Ex-act-ly!'

SCHRATZ, SCHWARZ and
WESTFALL-GREITER 2012: 77

The three vignettes reveal how the researchers themselves were affected by what their senses had perceived in their co-experiential experience of lived experience in the different contexts. In the narratives, attention is not only focused on verbal expressions and actions; the researchers also took into account non-propositional forms of experience, namely movements, gestures, looks, interactions, moods and atmospheres, which are expressed through facial expressions, gestures, tonality, rhythm and posture. Because of their pathic quality (Waldenfels 2004a), the vignettes capture these bodily experiences and thus give the data a particular richness.

In Vignette 3 ('On the pavement'), the interplay of the swinging pace, the forward and backward movement of the arms and the head moving back and forth appealed to the researcher as an ensemble of bodily experience and had a special meaning for him or her. The vignette is not about the young woman *per se*, but the experience of her appearance, which the researcher has co-experientially experienced in the situation described. Vignette 4 ('The principal on tour with her students') describes a moment during a field trip provided by the principal of a hospital school to newly arrived students that caught the researcher's attention; this is reflected in the richness of bodily experiences – their serious gazes, flicking heads, sparkling eyes, etc. – that the researcher co-experientially experienced. The researcher who wrote Vignette 5 ('Listening and reading in English class') used very different stylistic devices to recreate his or her co-experiential experience, in order to communicate the situation as vividly as possible in the description. Therefore, the art of writing vignettes is to express the sensuous aspect of things and condense the intersubjective experiences in the field to enable them to be experienced anew by readers (Agostini 2017: 26–9).

In contrast to other methodological approaches, vignette research is not about generalizable knowledge, but about making visible what seems significant to the researcher. The vignette is determined by the specificity of the situation, not the existence of a condition. 'Even a small event in a child's life is an event in that child's world and thereby a world event', argues Gaston Bachelard (1990: 33). The moments that researchers address are not subordinate to a typical general rule. It is only by passing through them that we can recognize the generality that is specific to them. Therefore, vignettes are characterized more by a particular accuracy and conciseness – in the sense of being pregnant, i.e. with meaning – than by precision. 'The vignette has a precision of a different kind. It is not precise in the sense of definitional claims. It is concise, i.e. pregnant' (Meyer-Drawe 2012a: 14).

The vignette is not precise in the sense of depicting in detail what actually occurred in the field with a view to measuring, weighing and counting it. That is not its intention. It is concise in the sense that it depicts the memorable, peculiar, pleasing, disturbing, curiosity-arousing aspects of a particular moment in a way that preserves the complexity, richness and vitality of such experiences. The vignette does not describe, it does not assert, it shows. This showing becomes vivid and points to a fullness or a surplus, as Käte

Meyer-Drawe (2011a) calls it, which is also contained in lived experience, and which is always more than we can explicitly put into words. Life experiences carry heavy traffic, so to a certain extent they can only be grasped experientially, as we have indicated with the different moments of experience with the apple tree (see 'Accessing the fragility of human action' section).

The researchers' co-experiential experience is initially recorded in experiential notes or protocols. Co-experiential journaling is challenging because experiences do not reveal themselves as such and yet have to be documented by the researcher. The resonance of an emotional experience also impresses itself on the researcher as a bodily experience. Therefore, the aforementioned seismographic attitude to perception is necessary for the holistic apprehension of experience, and the body serves as a memory aid. Researchers record memorable experiences that have a particularly striking bodily impact, as expressed in the three vignettes. In order to retain the sensory aspects of the comprehension of these formative moments, researchers should write the rough version of the vignette as soon as possible after the lived experience *in statu nascendi* and *in medias res* (in the midst of things). This capturing of immediate impressions brings about a special writing style that enables the density of holistic experiences to be expressed for the subsequent drafting process. Depending on the research location, the researchers try to find a timely opportunity to create a rough version of the vignette. Further information on how to write a first draft of a vignette is provided in chapter 3.

Responsivity as a virtue

Importantly in vignette research, the researcher and the research are inextricably locked together, and the role of the researcher becomes more diffuse in the tension between subjectivity and objectivity. For Michael Schratz and Rob Walker (1995) this blurs the demarcations between pure and applied, academic and practical, scholastic and immediately applicable research. They consider the role of the researcher in qualitative research to be unconventional:

Relinquishing claims to specialised expertise, being less clear about what aspects of the role are social and what are personal, lacking the security of stable paradigms and accepted methods throws the researcher back on personal resources; imaginative, cognitive and moral. As the insulation between the role and identity breaks down, so conventional values of objectivity, claims to truth and community of enquiry have to be rethought and reconstructed.

SCHRATZ and WALKER 1995: 5

This lack of security in the expertise of vignette researchers is due to the fact that they obtain their data from lived experience, which they cannot reflect on introspectively: 'A person cannot reflect on lived experience while living through experience' (Van Manen 1990: 10):

Lived experience is the starting point and end point of phenomenological research. The aim of phenomenology is to transform lived experience into a textual expression of its essence – in such a way that the effect of the text is at once a reflexive re-living and a reflective appropriation of something meaningful: a notion by which a reader is powerfully animated in his or her own lived experience.

Ibid.: 36

In vignette research, data are generated by the researcher *in* the experience itself, rather than obtained *from* the experience (see Figure 1). Whereas the participant-observer collects data, the vignette researcher is holistically involved, co-experiencing what is happening. This involvement makes them receptive to what occurs and able to capture the essence of the moment *in statu nascendi*. The essence is what makes the experience so significant for them. If a vignette shows how a child starts learning to ride a bike and suddenly succeeds in riding on two wheels without support, the essence would be the grasping of the very nature of riding a bike. It is impossible to predict the actual moment of this learning experience; it can only be reflected on retrospectively. The vignette is an instrument that helps capture such an experience with all the senses by co-experiencing it in as much detail as possible in order to grasp the essentials of it (in this case of riding the bike). The phenomenological question is not 'How does the child learn to ride the bike?' but it asks 'What is the nature or essence of the experience of learning?' (Van Manen 1990: 10).

This is what Waldenfels (2013a) calls an intermediate event (*Zwischenereignis*), which he does not see as an intentional action. He explains it as follows:

> I regard as an *intermediate* event something that, in happening, links up with something else in such a way that it responds to what the latter suggests and claims. . . . The order that emerges from these connections and intervenes to regulate them, I call responsive rationality. It embodies an open regulation, since what is ordered does not originate from this order itself. It regulates the way in which one responds to and engages with the unfamiliar.
>
> WALDENFELS 2013a: 50

With vignette research, the approach is at once broad and specialized: the vignette researcher does not limit him or herself to obtaining data from an angle or perspective that allows a problem to be fitted into a familiar and manageable pattern. Rather, it is precisely the unknown, the unfamiliar, that the researcher encounters in the lifeworld. In order to be open to this encounter with the unfamiliar and in the absence of research instruments for acquiring data, a distinctive phenomenological attitude is required. Vignette researchers adopt a phenomenological stance, bracketing assumptions, theories and understandings and remaining open to being affected by others' experiences. They go beyond observation and rely on their own senses, specifically attending to pathic elements such as facial and bodily expressions and tone of voice or silence, which they record in notes as a stream of experiential data. This experiential data is the primary source for writing up the experience in a phenomenological text.

For co-experiential experience in the research field, Waldenfels's insight (2013a) means that responsive experiences are fundamentally open-ended and cannot be captured with a ready-made instrument that directs the attention to specific questions and elicits the desired answers. To do justice to the principle of *epoché* (see 'Accessing the fragility of human action' section), researchers should also not let their perception be guided by theoretical presuppositions and prejudices and should allow space for intermediate events.

More attention needs to be paid to subjective perception in the research process because '[t]he reality is not interrogated, but experienced through the senses in certain contexts. Something catches our attention, it speaks to us, it takes on meaning for us. To write about it is not to record data, but to express perceptual experiences' (Meyer-Drawe 2020: 15). Engaging with this sensory quality of experience and the data derived from it to create vignettes requires a sharpening of perceptual sensitivity. To this end, in our research experience, collaborative engagement in a scientific community or professional learning community (PLC) has proven particularly useful for working on one's own sensory perception blind spots via collective feedback.

Figure 1 provides a simplified representation that compares and contrasts the phenomenological context of responsivity in vignette research with other empirical approaches to field research.

The different approaches and associated attitudes to field research in Figure 1 can be characterized as follows:

More directed approaches: From a distanced position, researchers usually seek data that derives from their research questions. They use either a checklist or list of questions to obtain the required data as precisely as possible, or they look out for data which prove their hypotheses. The people and objects observed serve as data sources for the researcher and are referred to as research objects or subjects.

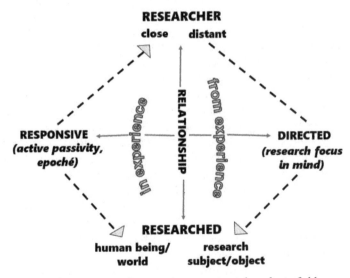

FIGURE 1 *Comparison of contrasting experiential modes in field research.*
Source: Authors

Unexpected experiences in the field tend to be confusing and are recorded as such in the field report to contextualize the process of data collection.

More responsive approaches: Researchers relate to the research field to gain the necessary proximity to what is happening. What is sought is not distance, but rather proximity, concern and responsivity. This closeness can also arise from everyday experience, which allows researchers to record details as a memory aid so that they can later write a vignette. It is necessary to weigh up how much fidelity to detail to aim for, to ensure that it does not detract from the description's conciseness and variety of meaning. 'Bracketing' theoretical presuppositions and prejudices in line with *epoché*, researchers respond with active passivity to what is happening in the field. Engagement with the world (people and objects) demonstrates asymmetric responsivity and takes place in response to an appeal (Lévinas 1992).

Figure 2 contrasts the two approaches. Whereas the relationship between the researcher and the researched is as close as possible in more responsive approaches, with directed approaches the distance is far greater.

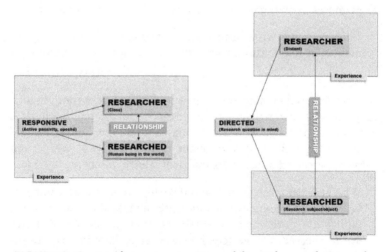

FIGURE 2 *Contrast between responsive and directed research approaches.*
Source: Authors

The social phenomenologist Ronald D. Laing (1967: 15–16) described the entangled nature of 'inter-experience' as the relation between my experience of you and your experience of me. While my experience is invisible to you and vice versa,

> I cannot avoid trying to understand your experience because although I do not experience your experience, . . . yet I experience you as experiencing. . . . I experience myself as experienced by you. And I experience you as experiencing yourself as experienced by me. And so on. The study of the experience of others is based on the inferences I make, from my experience of you experiencing me, about how you are experiencing me experiencing you experiencing me . . .
>
> LAING 1967: 16

Rosa's notion of resonance (2019) builds on Waldenfels's concept of responsivity, referring to 'a mode of being-in-the-world, i.e., a specific way of relating between the subject and the world' (Rosa 2019: 285). Resonance is characterized by its relation to response and means experiencing the world as responding. For Rosa, experiences of being-in-the-world and thus being in resonance can happen in the most diverse situations, namely in all situations where people are touched by something and addressed by something. Experiences of resonance are inherently unavailable; what is more,

> 'The encounter with the unavailable and the desire or struggle to make it available run through all areas of life like a leitmotif'.
>
> ROSA 2018: 8–9

Vignette researchers find themselves in this field of tension; that is, they enter the field to gain data but cannot gain it intentionally. It is precisely in the openness to the unplannable and unpredictable intermediate event that a resonant relationship can emerge and must be perceived as an opportunity or fruitful moment.

> Whether resonance occurs, and if so, how long it lasts, can never be predicted. Resonance is inherently unavailable, and it is like falling asleep: the more intensely we desire it, the less likely we are to succeed. Conversely, however, unavailability also means that the emergence of resonance can never be ruled out (again very like falling asleep). It can also occur in radically alienated or

adversarial circumstances, although this is of course unlikely. It is therefore a specific feature of resonance that it can be neither achieved nor prevented with any certainty.

Ibid.: 44

In Figure 1, this responsive relationship is contrasted with the directed approach. Sensory attention to human experience in the field escapes our direct initiative. It instead follows an 'intropathic sensing' (Busch and Därmann 2007), which happens preconsciously in the gap between 'pathos' and 'response' (Waldenfels 2002: 54–60). What awakens the researchers' attention and appeals to them takes on meaning for them. In the situational context, it is vital for the vignette researcher to sense these creative moments, respect them, give them space and time, and consider the uniqueness of the personal moment. The consequence of unavailability is that the researcher's attention cannot follow a predefined scheme as is the case with more directed approaches to field research (see Figure 1, right side). This makes it all the more important to help the bodily resonance in the vignette find expression by being responsive to it. The way to achieve this is described in detail in chapter 3.

Vignettes as a transformative force

Human coexistence consists of the experience of tension between stability and change. In the course of life, this experience enables us to establish routines that create security in our daily private and professional lives, so that we do not have to constantly think about the next steps to take. As corporeal experiences, they become deeply imprinted in our behaviour and influence what we do and how we do it. Accordingly,

> human beings load their experience with sense or meaning, although they are almost never explicitly conscious of doing so, especially when conducting life 'in the natural attitude'. Constitution is largely an activity that takes place in the background, apart from those instances where conscious decision-making takes place at the level of judgement.

MORAN 2015

From one point of view, routines create security, but from another, they can also reduce mindfulness in the present moment. If someone is very familiar with a situation, they do not have to pay much attention in order to act purposefully. For example, during a learner driver's first lesson a driving instructor has to draw attention to how to perform individual processes such as shifting gear, but once the learner has acquired more experience, the individual steps become automated – the learner has assimilated the behaviour. Learning and life experiences of this kind occur not only with regard to mechanical processes such as driving a car, but also in all formative experiences we have in life, because 'an experience is something from which one emerges changed' (Foucault 1996: 24). In vignette research, we aim to take a phenomenological attitude, making visible the transformational experiences inherent in everyday routines by co-experiencing people's experiences in their natural attitude.

When we explore experiences in the lifeworld with this phenomenological attitude, our co-experiential experience is affected and we emerge changed, as Michel Foucault (1996) suggests. In co-experiential experience, we are enmeshed in the natural attitude, which refers not only to thinking but also to the subject's entire relationship with the world, others, and itself (Koller 2018: 9). 'Lived experience is the breathing of meaning,' argues Van Manen (1990: 36), and accordingly vignette researchers are equally affected by their encounter with the lifeworld and lived experiences. Taking a phenomenological attitude, they explore the lifeworld as a phenomenon that typifies the human being-in-the-world.

Vignette research does not strive for answers to predetermined questions, but is a transformational process in which something known is experienced in an unknown way and the unknown becomes the known (Meyer-Drawe 2012a). What is meant by this is that the directing of attention to processes taking place in the here and now involves being taken hold of, which promotes an openness to new experiences. When you are taken hold of, your relationship to the world and to others also transforms your relationship to yourself (Krenn 2017), because 'every initiative includes a moment of creativity, the core of which, by its very nature, eludes mere derivation through circumstances; inventions create something new' (Fauser 2016: 175).

From a phenomenological point of view, the activities and actions set in routines are not actions that we anticipate, but responses to a call (solicitation) from things and our dialogue with them. For

Merleau-Ponty, our encounter in and with the (life)world does not take place on the basis of stimulus and response, but is a fleshy, sensuous intertwining (Merleau-Ponty 2009). Attempting to capture experiences *in statu nascendi* means that both researched and researchers are affected by the experience in the midst of the event. Neither can reflect on it as it occurs. Rather, experience is an event that one undergoes, and in the throes of experience it is impossible to simultaneously be participant and observer. Nonetheless the researcher has a particular stance in the field which directs his or her attention, and we deal with this in more detail in the section entitled 'Experiential protocols: noting your observations and perceptions'.

In order to get a holistic grasp of the experiences of the social world, when writing vignettes it is important to capture as many sense modalities as possible from the co-experiential bodily experience (see the section entitled 'The unavailability of everyday life/embodied subjectivity'). The phenomenologist's task here is not to explain co-experiential moments, but to disclose them (Langer 1989: 60), in order to arrive at 'the things themselves' (Husserl 2001: 168). To facilitate this process, Husserl (1962) introduced the notion of *epoché* – which we detailed in the 'Accessing the fragility of human action' section – the bracketing of preconceived opinions, prejudices, theoretical assumptions and scientific theses, in order to open up new perspectives and a new experiential space.

Referring to Husserl (2002: 42–6, 84, 101–3), Sara Heinämaa states (2019: 149) that 'the *epoché* of the lifeworld changes our relation to all worldly vocations and to all vocational life'. Suspending the assumptions, insights, and knowledge gained so far in life has a transformative power because it does something to the researcher:

> It does not suspend one interest for another but puts them all 'out of play' at the same time. The phenomenological attitude is not a temporary position that one can adopt and abandon at will. The change is permanent; no unaltered return to previous life is possible.
>
> HEINÄMAA 2019: 149

We cannot and do not intend to discuss the basic assumptions of descriptive phenomenology in depth here; vignette research is concerned with how to apply phenomenology's insights to practical situations. Books on research methods tend to be like manuals, consisting mainly of procedures and instructions to be followed. This approach does not work where the researcher himself or herself is the embodied 'tool' and has to fine-tune his or her perception. Rather than presenting the challenging and transformative nature of *epoché* as a tool in embodied research in action more generally, we invite you to read Vignette 6, 'Moving people', as a way of sharing in the author's co-experiential experience.

Vignette 6: 'Moving people'

> For the first session of the 'Creating Knowledge, Moving People' seminar, the leader has arranged the chairs into a circle. The students arriving separately in the room have hesitantly looked for a place and sat in it. Their gazes wander around the room, yet immediately turn to the seminar leader when his calm, quiet voice breaks the expectant silence: 'The starting point for our seminar is the challenging question, "How can we communicate scientifically relevant knowledge so that it gets under people's skin?"' A tense silence is felt in the room, and he invites the students to engage in an initial brainstorming session. Ideas bubble up loudly as if from a spring, back and forth across the circle, the students gesticulating, and their bodies moving animatedly and excitedly, their contributions filling the room with energy. Unnoticed, a student slowly rises and strides to the blackboard with a lunging step. He fumbles in the tray for a piece of chalk, raises it to the board, and thoughtfully writes in capital letters: 'IT'S A PITY PEOPLE ONLY NOTICE SILENCE WHEN YOU LEAVE.' He calmly walks toward the door and carefully pulls it shut behind him. Immediately the voices of those left in the room fall silent. Startled and disturbed, their eyes wander back and forth, affected and struck, between the stark farewell sentence on the board, the silent floor, and the bodies sitting in the circle.

> Revised version based on original in SCHRATZ 1994: 124

The writer of the vignette was obviously just as struck and affected in his co-experiential experience by the paradoxical intervention of the student who had left the room as the immediate addressees of the action, the seminar participants. While the other students are intensively and animatedly discussing the leader's question on the topic 'Creating Knowledge, Moving People', the 'parting sentence' on the board leaves the message that verbal discussion has its limits. His silence (*Schweigen*) is not perceived as a contribution to the discussion until he has left the room. It was only by shutting down the discussion and by walking out of it that he had an impact on the people in the room. 'Thus, one could say that the relationship of subjects undergoing a transformative educational process to the world and to themselves is negated, i.e., questioned, destabilised, or even completely invalidated, by certain problematic situations' (Koller 2018: 77).

The author of the vignette, in his phenomenological stance, was not concerned with reflecting on the possible epistemological gain of this intervention in theory or in terms of higher education teaching. Rather, he tried to let us, as readers of the vignette, participate as closely as possible in the event without having been there ourselves. He could also have written about how the seminar continued after the student left the room, for example, how the seminar leader dealt with the incident. The latter remains completely absent after his introduction in the vignette. Nevertheless, he is present – even to the reader of the vignette – in the setting described. In the process of writing it down, the vignette writer is guided by the impressions that affect him bodily. The phenomena that arise in his body determine what becomes visible in the vignette, i.e., comes to the fore, and what remains omitted recedes into the background.

Van Manen (1990: 54) addresses the reflective nature of all descriptions as transformations, noting that even 'life captured directly on magnetic or light-sensitive tape is already transformed at the moment it is captured. . . . So the upshot is that we need to find access to life's living dimensions while realizing that the meanings we bring to the surface from the depth of life's oceans have already lost the natural quiver of their undisturbed existence'. The vignette faces challenges common to all research that relies on human recall or recollection, whether qualitative or quantitative. Researchers must therefore be mindful that both their note-taking and their writing are acts of transformation. It goes without saying that capturing experiences for purposes of research is a complex task, in particular when human beings are involved in a particular social context. The impossibility of seeing the lifeworld with the eyes of others forces us to expose ourselves to the alien (Meyer-

Drawe 2010: 11). When we are required to understand the world through the eyes of the other, we can only make assumptions, we cannot experience it on somebody else's behalf. Therefore, in vignette research it is important to suspend the assumptions and prejudices with which we perceive others. Rather, we are confronted with strangeness, which shows itself in what we are confronted with.

When writing raw vignettes, vignette researchers are confronted with this strangeness. They bracket their own presuppositions, judgements and interpretations by virtue of their phenomenological attitude. The confrontation with the unfamiliar requires them to reorient their representation of the co-experiential experience. The pauses, the multiple attempts, the failed attempts, and the struggle to find meaningful expressions have a transformational effect by bracketing habitual attributions on the part of the vignette writer. Drafting the rough version of a vignette is an experimental activity within the research process, as the writer has to 'disconnect' and try something new. As a result, he or she finds himself or herself in a role that Foucault aptly describes as follows (1996: 24): 'I am an experimenter in the sense that I write in order to change myself and no longer think the same as before.'

The deployment of *epoché* is further sharpened in the PLC or research group. At this stage, the raw vignette is initially presented to the protected collegiate space via resonance reading and feedback (see 'Presenting your raw vignette' and 'Resonance reading' sections). Since the participants in the feedback were not themselves in the role of co-experiencers, to sharpen the representation of what was perceived, they ask how things became apparent to the vignette writer, for instance: 'Was the voice hesitant?' 'Or was it more brittle?' 'Or soft?' By asking questions, it is possible to get even closer to the experience as it appeared in the event and to present it as concisely as possible in the vignette. The participants give feedback on the raw vignette from different perspectives, on the one hand by revealing their personal bodily resonance with the vignette, and on the other by asking questions and questioning individual formulations that imply interpretation, forcing the author to present the experience more precisely.

Scenic representations, where the vignette writer acts out (part of) the event, can help describe how something was revealed to them (Agostini, Peterlini and Schratz 2019; Peterlini 2017). Scenic representation has the advantage of not requiring words to describe co-experiential experience. Having to choose words is limiting, whereas scenic representation can draw on the full range of bodily expressions. The body can express more than spoken or written words can.

For example, in the expository session with Vignette 6, 'Moving people', participants might ask for details about how the student left the room. The vignette writer takes on the role of the student from memory and depicts how he walked from the blackboard to the door and closed the door behind him. Based on this tangible co-experiential experience, participants can offer their own verbalizations to refine the text. According to Hannah Arendt (1960), something collectively new may emerge from joint discussion that may be of particular social relevance in the future. This is particularly the case with vignette research because discussion through resonance reading is always done collectively in a shared research community (see 'Presenting your raw vignette' and 'Resonance reading' sections). In our joint discussions about vignettes, new common development opportunities have repeatedly become apparent to us. Vignette 6 ('Moving people') could thus also contribute to the resonance reading (see 'Resonance reading' section), highlighting the power of the word and the powerlessness of silence and vice versa.

Related approaches

As readers of this publication, you have already learned a lot about vignette research. However, we have not yet provided an overview of what is special about our specifically phenomenological approach. We will thus now try to distinguish it from related research approaches. What, for example, are the differences between descriptive phenomenological and ethnographic research, which are often considered very similar? And what are the differences between the vignette approach and other approaches within descriptive phenomenology? Questions of demarcation also arise with regard to casuistry/case studies and narrative research/enquiry. There are not always unambiguous answers to these questions. There is no such thing as one phenomenology, ethnography or casuistry; different fields and disciplines adopt a range of positions and approaches. At the risk of simplification, the 'Phenomenological research' section is an attempt to classify phenomenological vignettes and differentiate them from other approaches, whilst simultaneously acknowledging the significant similarities and overlaps between the methodologies.

Descriptive Phenomenological research

Vignette research borrows from the phenomenological method of exemplary description (e.g. Brinkmann 2011; Lippitz 1987). As such, they are 'short, concise narratives that capture moments of experience' (Schratz, Schwarz and Westfall-Greiter 2012: 34). These concise narratives have very specific characteristics (e.g. length, use of the second-person perspective, and a particular understanding of experience), which enrich the text itself. According to Wilfried Lippitz (1987), exemplary description is the preferred procedure in phenomenology.

The exemplary descriptive method is influenced in its genesis by Husserl's transcendental phenomenology, and his analyses of the intentionality and horizonality of experience (Buck 1989: 60–2). However, Husserl's successors modified the method, understanding subjectivity as a bodily consciousness that is not centred on the subject but is intersubjectively constituted (Lippitz 1987: 116). Similarly to other phenomenological approaches, vignettes 'aim to gather pre-reflexive experiential accounts' (Van Manen 2016: 311). However, researchers have to realize that experiential accounts or descriptions of lived experience are never truly identical to the pre-reflexive lived experiences themselves. All descriptions of experiences are already transformations of those experiences. According to Van Manen (2016: 313), '[w]ithout this dramatic elusive element of lived meaning to our reflective attention, phenomenology would not be necessary'. In addition, researchers writing phenomenological vignettes need to adopt the descriptive phenomenological attitude, seeing, thinking and expressing as described in the reduction (*Rückführung*). Reflective methods of vignette reading to draw out and analyse meaning also need to be integrated with *epoché* and phenomenological reduction (see the sections entitled 'Accessing the fragility of human action' and 'The phenomenological attitude').

From a Husserlian perspective, the reflective methods deployed by the human sciences are concerned with identifying the major and minor eidetic themes associated with the phenomena or events that are being studied in phenomenological research projects. However, work with vignettes, whose theoretical grounding rests on Merleau-Ponty's embodied phenomenology, assumes that the reduction of the modes of reality (*Gegebenheitsweisen*) will always be incomplete due to the bodily constitution of human consciousness (Agostini 2016a: 36). Vignette writers are aware of the limits imposed on them by their bodily reference to the specifics of 'being-in-the-world' ('*être au monde*', Merleau-Ponty 2009). 'Being-in-the-world' (ibid.) is accompanied by the perspective of experience and the difference between the subject and the world that the subject perceives. The renunciation of the completeness of transcendental reduction is justified by emphasizing humans' nature as experiential beings:

> The most important lesson which the reduction teaches us is the impossibility of a complete reduction. This is why Husserl is constantly re-examining the possibility of the reduction. If we were absolute mind, the reduction would present no problem. But since, on the contrary, we are in the world, since indeed our reflections are carried out in the temporal flux on which we are trying to seize (since they *sich einströmen*, as Husserl says), there is no thought which embraces all our thought.
>
> MERLEAU-PONTY 2009: XV

Phenomenological approaches explore examples and varieties of lived experience, for instance in the form of vignettes but also in the form of other accounts of lived experience. The lifeworld, the world of everyday lived experience, is both the source and the object of phenomenological research. Any part of the lifeworld can be investigated to gain material relating to lived experience: through co-experiential experience, observation, interview or fictional accounts (Van Manen 1979). '[T]he aim is to collect examples of possible human experiences in order to reflect on the meanings that may inhere in them' (Van Manen 2016: 313). Hence, the patterns of meaning of one's own experiences are also potentially the experiences of others and therefore may be recognizable by others.

Anecdotal research

Phenomenological anecdotes are a frequently and variously used approach. Anecdotes are mostly understood in everyday language to be short, entertaining stories, often oral, about true events. Van Manen uses anecdotes in connection with observations – in this form they are similar to the vignette – but he points out that personal experience and interviews can also be the basis for anecdotes (1990: 69). He describes his form of anecdote as a 'narrative device that is concrete and taken from life (in a fictional or real sense) and that may be offered as an "example" in a phenomenological sense' (2016: 250). He defines the narrative structure of the anecdote as 'a very short and simple story' (Van Manen 2016: 252), describing 'a single incident', beginning 'close to the central moment of experience', including 'important concrete details', containing 'several quotes (what was said, done, and so on)', concluding 'quickly after the climax or when the incident has passed', and having 'an effective or "punchy" last line: it creates punctum' (ibid.).

Another branch of the Innsbruck school of thought, the Innsbruck anecdotal research group, describes the anecdote as 'a memorable story in which events with a special impact are pointedly condensed, and in which they are recounted to the researcher ... from the memory of the experience' (Rathgeb, Krenn and Schratz 2017: 130). The initial aim of anecdotal research in Austria was to investigate learning processes over longer periods of time. Discussions with students about their four years of schooling at Austrian secondary schools formed the basis of the anecdotes and represent a rich source for researchers investigating memories of learning as an experience. Writing anecdotes is not about the exact depiction of details, but rather about condensing the affective, disturbing, astonishing or surprising aspects of conversation in such a pithy way that the experiences revealed in the conversation sound new and become comprehensible for readers. This is achieved by taking in not only *what* is being said, but also *how* it is said. Does a pupil stammer and falter while telling a story? Do words keep failing her or do they just gush out? Does the interlocutor lower his head or turn his gaze away? (Ibid.). Hence, like vignettes, anecdotes place a strong focus on bodily articulation and its translation into language (through metaphors and figures of speech). Similar to vignette researchers, anecdotal researchers of the Innsbruck school of thought have to adopt a co-experiential attitude. Hence, data is collected via interviews, but with the co-experiential dimensions of vignette research. This is based on the assumption that the inquisitive experiential attitude gives researchers access to the experiences of others that would not be accessible in any other way. The experiences contained in anecdotes are to be understood – as are vignettes – as incisive examples that go beyond the specifics, illuminating the general or universal and providing new perspectives. Furthermore, a questioning and open approach is taken to the analysis of the texts: as with vignettes, readings of anecdotes attempt to do justice to the ambiguity of experiences rather than to define them in an ultimately valid way.

As with vignettes, raw anecdotes are discussed with a (research) group and, if necessary, the participants in the situation, and are subsequently enriched and condensed. During intersubjective validation, participants are asked to describe the situation from their own point of view. The anecdote or vignette writers always retain control of the narrative – after all, it is their intersubjective experience. At this stage of the process, the account can be supplemented with contextual information or quotes, or corrected if necessary. The aim of validation is not to reconstruct the experience as a whole, searching for the 'truth' of a case, but rather to clarify the language and the experiential context. However, whereas vignettes are understood as a means to experience moments of (extra-)curricular learning, anecdotes in the Innsbruck tradition are seen as an opportunity to record remembered moments of (extracurricular) learning. Hence, vignettes are momentary, while anecdotes may extend over a broader time period. Vignettes are based purely on observations in the sense of perceptions and co-experiential experiences, while anecdotes supplement observations with interactional verbal exchanges.

Narrative research/inquiry

Vignettes contain narrative elements and can be seen as narrative tools. However, *narrative research* or *inquiry* – the two terms are used differently depending on the authors, but generally interchangeably – must be defined more broadly as exploring and conceptualizing personal experiences, with the aim of exploring in depth the meanings people assign to their experiences. It can encompass a range of approaches such as phenomenology, but also ethnography, grounded theory, narratology, action research, and literary analysis (Salkind 2010). It is a form of inquiry where participants have a great deal of control over the process of qualitative research (Holloway and Freshwater 2007). However, there is no consensus about the nature and structure of narrative research in general (Ollerenshaw and Creswell 2002). Narrative is seen as 'both phenomenon and method' (Connelly and Clandinin 1990).

On the one hand, the concept of 'narrative' contains a multiplicity of meanings, and on the other hand, it is a generic term, which makes specific definitions difficult. Some writers (e.g. Labov and Waletzky 1967: 12) require narratives to have specific elements such as an abstract (summary of the narrative), orientation (time, location and participants), a complicating action and its evaluation, and a final resolution; while others (e.g. Elliot 2005) see this as too prescriptive for an approach to story analysis. Elements that are common to all narratives and should be connected are described by Immy Holloway and Dawn Freshwater (2007: 4) as 'a plot, a stated problem and a cast of characters'. Hence, like vignettes, narratives pay attention to time, place, plot and scene, although not (as strongly) to embodied experiences. Michael Connelly and Jean Clandinin (1990) name storytelling as a key element, along with metaphors, specific particularities and folk knowledge. Like a vignette, a narrative 'adds creative, aesthetic and craft elements, but it also enhances practice. Its main strength lies in its communicative power and its immediacy. Researchers participating in it also engage their emotions, and they are not neutral or distant but empathic and close to the narrators' (Holloway and Freshwater 2007: 3) – even if they are not co-experiencing the experiences of the participants as in vignette research. Furthermore, like vignette researchers, narrative researchers work with small samples of participants to obtain rich, contextual descriptions and free-ranging discourse. The emphasis is on related experience, which gives rise to the most frequent criticisms of narrative (and vignette) research, namely, that narrative stresses the individual over the social context.

Generally, narrative research/inquiry takes the form of interviews with people on the topic or theme of interest, but it also involves the analysis of written documents such as journal records, letters, (auto-)biographical writing, lesson plans and newsletters, or shared experiences through participant observation (Connelly and Clandinin 1990). However, in contrast to vignette research, it must be stated that there is a stronger collaboration with participants on the generation of the text. Whereas in narrative research/inquiry participants sometimes produce their own stories (spoken life stories, or photographic self-portraits, day-by-day journals of events, descriptions of personal experiences, drawings of a family tree), in vignette writing the text is always crafted by the researcher. However, in vignette research the participants may ultimately be pertinently included in the writing process in the resonance reading phase (see 'Presenting your raw vignette' and 'Resonance reading' sections), in order to craft the final vignette. In conclusion, it must be acknowledged that there is more to the study of narrative than the phenomenological approach. Narrative researchers differ in particular in how they retell or rewrite the narratives of the participants in their research – or recreate their stories – sometimes going through a process of interpretation (Holloway and Freshwater 2007). Vignette researchers seek to refrain from interpretation in vignettes, whereas narrative researchers actively seek interpretation in order to enrich specific aspects of the understanding of phenomena.

Casuistic research/case study research

The term 'casuistry' – from the Latin 'casus' for case – originated in law and Christian moral theology and is considered, generally, to focus on individual cases in a particular field (Wensierski 2006: 260). Though the wide variety of terms associated with it is confusing – 'case study', 'case analysis', 'case method', 'case presentation', 'case history', 'case description', 'case reconstruction', 'case work' or 'case report' are some examples – it is not always clear whether the term refers primarily to the practical work on the case or the scientific effort to acquire knowledge. Thus, quite different practices have evolved for dealing with cases in different academic fields and teaching traditions.

One fundamental distinction that can be made is between casuistry as a research tool and casuistry as a training medium. In both roles, casuistry is very popular not only in psychoanalysis or jurisprudence, but also in medicine, psychology, psychiatry, bioethics and education. Casuistry appears to be the ideal way to provide researchers and students with an introduction to practical problems that is both theoretically based and relevant to practice, and which, by addressing the tension between the general and the particular (e.g. Wernet 2006: 189; see also Barthel 2010), also has promising potential to link research and teaching. This tends to derive from 'cases' that are prepared in such a way as to enable learning to take place 'on the case' (e.g. Schuhmann 2017: 10; Steiner 2014: 6–9). However, in the course of the demarcation we must critically note that in the context of casuistry, the terms 'case', 'example', 'case study', 'example case', and also 'understanding' and 'learning' are often used without being defined or differentiated with regard to context. Moreover, casuistry deals with features that in other understandings (see, for example, Kant 1797: 479–80, § 52 (FN) [A 167]) can only be attributed to the example in question. In contrast, Günther Buck, along with Immanuel Kant and others, makes a strict distinction between 'case' and 'example' (Buck 1989: 61–118; see also Buck 1967). According to this, the case would merely be an illustration of a general phenomenon, so it has 'the function of direct representation' (Buck 1989: 139); in the example, however, it is the particular features of the example that are of interest, bringing to mind the general through 'the "illustration" peculiar to the example' (ibid.); the knowledge derived from it can thus always also be related to analogous facts (ibid.).

Phenomenological vignettes, as exemplary descriptions, aim – similarly to casuistic approaches – to express the general in terms of the specific, but without generalizing or subsuming (for example, see Buck 1989: 166; for casuistic approaches see, e.g., Müller, 1995: 99).'The phenomenological notion of "example" is methodologically a unique semiotic figure for phenomenological inquiry' (Van Manen and Van Manen 2021: 17). In their narrative condensation, they illustrate (aesthetic) perception and experience 'by example' (and not 'by case'), but without claiming – as many casuistic approaches do – to reconstruct or depict reality, rather evoking or recalling it – bringing it back, summoning experience – bringing experience vividly to life (Agostini 2020a: 171–3). For example, well-written and well-edited vignettes may give the writer and reader the experience of presence, closeness, propinquity or proximity in place and time. In this sense, vignettes are examples that depict a specific relationship between the particular and the general/universal, whereby the general/universal, into which the particular is subsumed, must first be traced (ibid.).

Critical incident/key incident research

In addition to the term 'case' in the context of casuistry or case study research, the terms 'critical incidents' and 'key incidents' are also used, with the latter term, in contrast to the former, being understood as more value-neutral (Lindow 2013: 56). But what exactly is meant by a 'critical incident'?

> A critical incident need not be spectacular: it suffices that it should hold significance. As such, at the individual level, it can be events or circumstances that made one stop and think, perhaps revisit one's assumptions, or impacted one's personal and professional learning. At the collective level, it can be a systemic problem resulting from organizational maladaptation, or an issue arising from differences among stakeholders. In short, an incident may be defined as critical when the action(s) taken contributed to an effective or an ineffective outcome. At heart, all incidents pertain to matters such as culture, knowledge, competence, relationships, beliefs, emotions, communication, or treatment.
>
> SERRAT 2017: 1078

Such moments may be perceived as positive or negative. Hence, critical incident or key incident research – it is also referred to as critical incident method or technique – are used in a variety of (research) fields as well as on different levels. The critical incident method is mostly attributed to John Flanagan and it is considered 'a systematic, open-ended technique that involves analyzing specific situations to determine which communicative actions or behaviors would lead to the best possible outcome of a given situation' (Allen 2017). The critical incident method can be employed in a variety of ways such as observations or in-depth, descriptive interviews. There is currently some debate on the nature of this approach. It is not clear if it is a method for data collection and analysis or a comprehensive research methodology.

Roderik F. Viergever (2019) argues that it is a methodology, because often key methodological dimensions are described and it has a clear focus. Studies that apply this technique make use of various methods for data collection and analysis and the use of a specific format for those methods is described, explained, evaluated and justified. The implication is that philosophical and practical assumptions and studies using the critical incident method cannot easily make use of additional methodologies simultaneously. Similar to vignettes, critical incidents aim to generate learning experiences and can provide a rich, personal perspective on life that facilitates understanding of the issues and obstacles people face from time to time. Hence, in both approaches a practical problem can occur, which requires a (theoretically justified) solution. However, unlike vignettes, critical incident research illuminates avenues for improvement or replication if outcomes are effective (Serrat 2017: 1078). Hence, the aim of critical incident researchers is to understand the critical requirements for individuals, processes or systems. In contrast, vignette researchers have a more differentiated concept of experience, being interested in the process of experience itself and looking to explore its meanings – before the application of any particular interpretation.

Ethnographic research

Ethnographic research involves the descriptive study of particular human societies and their social relations. It is interested in the diversity of culture at home or abroad. It is often based on fieldwork, requiring the complete immersion of the researcher in the culture and everyday lives of the people who are the subject of the study. Ethnography is the primary method of social and cultural anthropology, and it is integral to the social sciences and humanities in general. For these reasons, ethnographic studies relate to many fields of study and many kinds of personal experience – including community-based or international internships. Probably the best-known ethnographic method is that of participant observation.

The question is how this form of methodological access, which was introduced by the founder of modern ethnology, Bronislaw Malinowski, in the 1920s as the (preferred) method of ethnography, can be distinguished from co-experiential experience. Similar to co-experiential experience, participatory observation (comparable to what is known as shadowing, in which investigators follow those they are investigating wherever they go) is an approach that attempts to situate and open up the structures and horizons of meaning of the participants in the field (Lamnek 2010: 498; Schulz 2010: 171). However, a phenomenological approach places the emphasis clearly on the processes of creating and forming meaning, i.e. the genesis of the meaning that objects and humans have in the everyday world and through which something is experienced and perceived as that something (Lippitz 1987: 110; Waldenfels 2000: 95). In order to approach the lifeworld, phenomenology brackets the question of being, of what is subjective and what is objective, and assumes an interconnectedness with the phenomena of the lifeworld that presupposes all objectification. Ethnography, in contrast, focuses its gaze more intensively than phenomenology on the reconstruction of social settings and (cultural) structures or on the social and individual construction of the subject rather than on processes of meaning formation and sense-making (Brinkmann 2011: 75; Stieve 2010: 28–31). Thus, an ethnographic approach is committed to the modern understanding of the subject, which sees the sovereign subject as the starting point of the constitution of the world and thus refers to constructivist ways of thinking; phenomenology, on the other hand, speaks of a bodily situated, non-autonomous yet pathic being anchored in the world, which allows us as humans to be affected. The aim of both approaches is to participate in everyday situations or in the everyday world of the people at the centre of the study in order to explore their patterns of interaction, values and meanings and to document them for scientific evaluation.

Essential characteristics of both approaches are thus the immersion of the researchers in the field under investigation, their influence on what they observe through their participation in the situation, and their view of the participating individuals or, from a phenomenological point of view, of the world as it appears to them (Flick 2005: 206; Stieve 2010: 25). What they also have in common is an underlying approach that consciously allows researchers to be alienated as they question familiar bodies of knowledge, paving the way for the discovery of the unfamiliar and of new aspects and perspectives. In both approaches, the focus is on a critical distance from and control of habitual tendencies and basic assumptions, as well as palpable respect for the uniqueness of each individual. Further similarities can be found in the way they approach logging and writing, which are subject to selection processes and are understood less as the exact reproduction of what happened than as a constant process of transformation (Lüders 2000: 396). In both ethnographic and phenomenological research strategies, data collection and evaluation are not strictly separated. Moreover, minutes and field notes are not regarded as finished transcriptions, but are supplemented, modulated and reformulated by new experiences and texts, resulting in a new, condensed description.

Usually, an ethnographic approach is connected with a stronger standardization of the situation of the observer, with the aim of achieving a stronger objectification of the data (Cloos 2010). But even in ethnography, there is no observation guide that will guarantee so-called equal attention *(gleichschwebende Aufmerksamkeit)* – an openness in which the observers are receptive to all the expressions and reactions of the participants and that therefore is closely related to the basic phenomenological attitude of *epoché*. In contrast to phenomenological approaches, ethnographic approaches place the theoretical emphasis on cultural meanings (Hitzler 2000: 17). Further differences arise with regard to research focus: while ethnography is often case-oriented (Flick 2005: 206–7) and thus places the individual at the centre of interest, phenomenology is primarily oriented towards the phenomena that occur in the course of experience. Particularly because of the different understandings ethnography and phenomenology have of the subject, the methods of co-experiential experience and participant observation differ significantly in terms of researchers' attitude and approach. While, as the names already make clear, participant observation proceeds observationally – which implies a distanced attitude or a distanced view of artificial unfamiliarity with the observed (Hirschauer and Amann 1997: 12) – vignette researchers' pre-predicative and pre-reflexive entanglement with the objects of interest leads them to be described as co-experiential experiencers. In vignette research, it is often researchers' own experiences that become the starting point of a co-experiential experience. In addition, vignettes are understood on the basis of one's own pre-conventional experiences.

Both co-experiential experience and participant observation can give rise to what are known as thick or dense descriptions (Geertz

1991). However, phenomenological vignettes are texts that should be evocative, aiming to allow their readers to experience an emotional and ethical response. Van Manen (2016: 241) underlines that there is a relation between the written structure of a text and the evocative effects that it may have on the reader. The more evocative a text, the more strongly meaning is embedded within it; hence, the more difficult it is to paraphrase or summarize the text and the felt understandings embedded within it. The evocative aspects of vignettes also involve an aesthetic imperative and concise language that is an authentic expression of the world rather than speaking about it. Moreover, the language of vignettes must be pathic, referring to the immediate presence and feeling of experience, able to involve the emotions, the body, the pathic and the pathically inspired. Therefore, a (research) group is needed, which constantly questions the words of the texts, and also their meanings, in order to literally condense them.

Table 1 summarizes the explanations of the related approaches.

TABLE 1 Similarities with and differences from vignette research

Research methodology	Similarities/areas of overlap with vignette research	Distinctive/unique features of vignette research
Descriptive phenomenological research	• Borrows from the phenomenological method of exemplary description • Intersubjectivity is fundamental • Aims to gather pre-reflexive experiential accounts • Employs phenomenological attitude (*epoché* and phenomenological reduction)	• Specific instances of descriptive phenomenological research • Specific texts with specific characteristics
Anecdotal research	• Borrows from the phenomenological method of exemplary description • Co-experiential experience is fundamental • Strong focus on bodily articulations and their translation into language (through metaphors and figures of speech) • Communicative, intersubjective validation process in the group as necessary	• Co-experiential experiences (without accounts of recalled experiences or questions and answers to collect more data) *in medias res* • Reports on a specific moment in time, rather than a broader time frame
Narrative research/ inquiry	• Captures personal experiences • Collects individual stories • Rich, contextual descriptions • Attention to time, place, plot and scene • Empathic and close to the participants	• Co-experiences the experience of others rather than reporting or observing • Rich descriptions of *embodied* experience • Less collaboration with participants on text generation: In narrative research/inquiry participants sometimes produce their own stories

Casuistic research/ case study research	• Narrative and illustrative • Something general/universal is depicted through a specific, concrete scene • Aims to address the discrepancy between theory and practice • Used in the context of reflection on practice and research • Used in research instruments and professionalization tools	• Learning 'by example' instead of learning 'by case' • Visualization (*Vergegenwärtigung*) instead of reconstruction
Critical incident/ key incident research	• Interested in experiences • Practical problems occur, which require (theoretically based) solutions • Conflict situations or everyday moments (positive or negative events)	• Can be part of a specific research approach or an independent methodology • Differentiated concept of experience in vignette research
Ethnographic research	• Participation in everyday situations or in the everyday world • Immersion of the researchers in the field under investigation and their influence on what is observed through their participation in the situation • Interested in the view of participating individuals • Thick description of a situation • Focus on the unfamiliar and strangeness	• Co-experiential experiences, rather than participant observations, pre-reflexive entanglement vs. distant attitude • Foregrounds moments of the experiential situation that are 'pregnant-with-meaning' and pathic • Strong focus on linguistic condensation (partly literary due to metaphors and linguistic images) • Strong focus on group work

Source: Authors

CHAPTER TWO

Characteristics of the Vignette Research Process

After discussing the key concepts underlying the development of vignette research as well as its methodological foundations, the question arises as to how the research process is actually conducted. What specific attitude does vignette research require on the part of researchers? What challenges does it pose, including in online settings? How can researchers gain intersubjective access to the experiences of others? This chapter provides you with an experiential response to these questions through concrete examples, drawing readers into the process of vignette research and allowing them to experience it first-hand, as it were. The chapter will give you insights into how it will feel to approach something phenomenologically and how to adopt the phenomenological attitude of a co-experiential position. It is also important to observe certain ethical and quality criteria, some of which are different for vignette research from those that are known from other approaches. At the end of the chapter you will find ethical guidelines and quality criteria, which can be used to check whether researchers comply with the quality standards of vignette research.

The phenomenological attitude

Vignette 7: 'Sabine and "Nighttime I" by Richard Oelze'

Sabine joins two girls who are making their leisurely way through the ground floor. She follows them through the basement up to the extension wing, then suddenly starts: 'It's in the other room,' she remarks briefly, rather more to herself than to the other two. Abruptly she turns on her heel and quickly turns left towards the ground floor, which is labelled 'The Early Years: Art after 1945'. She stops in front of Richard Oelze's work *Nachtzeit I* (Nighttime I), created around 1949. The slim young woman stands in front of the small, dark picture, then steps back, unfolds her chair, sits down, and leans forward. Leaning forward, she stares motionlessly and tensely at the picture from about two meters away. Then she drops her shoulders. Her gaze descends to her lap, and she makes notes with her pencil. Then she gets up, walks with her clipboard and sheets of paper very close to the sign with details about the work, takes a look at the title of the picture, and then stands very close to the work. Her eyes wander over it. Mrs Hennah and Anne walk past her; Sabine turns her head in their direction, a smile crosses her face. She sits down in her chair again. Sabine crosses one leg over the other, alternately looks at the information about the work and her A4 sheets, and writes. She straightens the papers and puts them back on the clipboard. Then she gets up and repeatedly brings her face very close to the work. With her clipboard in her hand, she plumps down on her chair. She takes a coloured pencil from her box and lets the box slide gently onto the floor at her feet. She draws. A man in gloves and a woman in high heels walk past her, talking loudly. The high heels go clickety-clack. Sabine's head remains motionless, hanging downwards. Her eyes are glued to the sheet.

BUBE 2022: 165[1]

Vignettes can draw our attention to the fact that humans are always doing more than merely taking a neutral view of an immobile and well-ordered reality. As corporeal beings, they are by no means mere subjects facing a supposedly objective world head-on. Rather, they find themselves in a world that they can hear, smell, touch, see and taste. They are immersed in a world that they perceive with all their senses and which enables them to have experiences from which they emerge changed (Foucault 1996). They always perceive experience as a specific event in their interaction with the world; the object they perceive (facts) and their perception of it (mode of access) cannot be separated from each other (Waldenfels 1992). Hence, depending on their perspective, different things come into focus and into view. In the vignette at the beginning of this chapter (Vignette 7), this is illustrated by Sabine in the museum and her reaction to a work entitled 'Nighttime I'. In the beginning, the 'slim young woman stands in front of the small, dark picture', then she 'steps back, unfolds her chair, sits down, and leans forward'. Afterwards, 'she gets up, walks with her clipboard and sheets of paper very close to the sign with details about the work, takes a look at the title of the picture, and then stands very close to the work.' As readers, you don't know what the young woman is thinking, but you can interpret her movements and read her body expression. You might be triggered by the vignette, feel something that you are not yet able to identify in detail or put into words.

You might be irritated by what happens to Sabine. How do you experience Sabine's experience? How does the artwork appear to you? How did the experience affect others around you? Did it trigger anything else? If it is outside of what you know and you cannot grasp it is because it invalidates your previous assumptions, it constitutes a pathic experience as defined by Waldenfels (2007), an affect that can bring about an experience. In phenomenology, pathos (*Widerfahrnis*), being affected by the world and by others, events and experiences, is closely related to the concept of corporeality in which rationality and emotions are inseparable.

The vignette can be read in different ways. It seems through Sabine's movements that she adopts very different perspectives; at one point she stares at the picture from close up, at another she takes it in from a distance. The vignette also reveals a perhaps unexpected moment of sensory response and attention. Sabine is so absorbed in the work that she no longer notices two museum visitors passing by. Sabine's facial expressions, gestures and posture reveal a particular level of engagement.

The short scene was recorded by a vignette researcher in the form of notes or what are known as 'experiential minutes' or 'experiential protocols' (*Erfahrungsprotokolle*) at the moment Sabine was gripped, and the raw vignette was subsequently discussed by a (research) group or community of practice in the form of resonance reading (see 'Presenting your raw vignette' and 'Resonance reading' sections) and then condensed linguistically into a vignette. Just like Sabine, the vignette writer was magically attracted by the process of experiencing, by the gloominess of the image and especially by Sabine's increasing attention and concentration. A moment of co-affiliation (*Koaffizierung*) occurred that allowed the researcher to share in Sabine's experiences in the museum. Vignette researchers select scenes – like the one around Sabine – which they condense into phenomenological texts in the form of exemplary description (Lippitz 1987) – according to what affects them as co-experiencers. But what does it actually mean to be affected by something? And what is it that affects researchers as humans that is able to touch their senses? Usually it is something that catches their eyes, their ears or their nose that stands out from what is usual and familiar, that stands out and yet connects to their (pre- or unconscious) previous experiences. Hence, in the field, vignette writers – and not only Sabine in the vignette – adopt a very specific point of view; depending on their proximity or distance from the scene of experience, they perceive differently. Thus, depending on the vignette writer's perspective and situatedness, the clatter of high heels can be perceived as quieter or louder. But as well as the situation, this depends on individuals' previous experiences or current interests; something can be perceived as something else.

Husserl has highlighted that experience is inconceivable without prior anticipatory experience. Therefore, as something to be perceived or understood at all, a new experience must always occur against the background of the previous horizon of experience. Thus, every experience is actually experiential (Buck 1989). Experiences in vignettes or by vignette writers in the field never start from scratch *per se*, but are based on what is already there. In this sense, prior knowledge and prior experience are the conditions for perceiving and experiencing anything at all. At the same time, prior knowledge is inevitably accompanied by a perspective. Thus, the bodily situatedness of perceiver and perceived are a condition of perception and this is of central significance for phenomenological research.

The phenomenological method, therefore, requires a change of attitude on the part of the perceiver, namely to suspend the 'pre-philosophical' (*vorphilosophische*) or 'natural attitude' (*natürliche Einstellung*), in which researchers are absorbed in objects and naively assume that a reality exists independently of their perception or mode of accessing it. Only by suspending this assumption can the goal of expanding one's own sphere of perception and experience be achieved (Husserl 1962: 154; 1973: 66). In a first step, the validity of the world and thus the pre-judgement of an implicitly presupposed transcendence of the natural world is bracketed by means of *epoché* (from Greek: stopping, inhibition, holding back, see also the 'Accessing the fragility of human action' section). Hence, the basic phenomenological attitude of *epoché* initially requires the suspension or bracketing of hasty judgement or any final decision. Then in the second step – phenomenological reduction – researchers reflect sceptically on the relationship between the object of perception and its perceivers: The 'content' of the percept leads them back to the perceptual style of the perceiver. But what does that mean in concrete terms?

On the one hand, researchers try to understand the experiences they encounter in their lifeworld: their exploratory, pre-scientific experience of the world that acts as the self-evident, unquestioned basis for their everyday thinking and acting. However, on the other hand, they must not be wholly absorbed in these worlds of experience, otherwise, they will no longer be able to reflect on them adequately. In concrete terms, this means a suspension of the unreflected knowledge and opinions of the lifeworld so that vague preconceptions and pre-understandings that affect certain phenomena, for example, based on their own experiences, come to light but are also suspended. This approach breaks with experience-based bias and allows researchers to distance themselves, taking the first step towards becoming more aware of their entanglement with phenomena as they then take the second step and reflect (Agostini 2016a: 35–9; Agostini and Peterlini 2023).

Only by undertaking *epoché* and phenomenological reduction can researchers become aware of their own sense-giving role, through which the objective of this methodical approach, the expansion of their sphere of experience, can come about at all. Only in this way does subjectivity emerge as the instance that constitutes the condition of the possibility of any phenomenon. This enables the world to come into view as a constituted world of a constituting bodily consciousness and enables phenomena to be perceived in the way they appear to the perceiver.

'To perceive otherwise is to perceive differently,' remarks Lévinas (1983: 156). By being perceived in a particular way, an object appears in the researcher's experience as a particular object. That an object appears as a determinate object does not mean that it is a determinate object, but that it becomes a determinate object by acquiring meaning and thus is able to reveal itself as a determinate object in the first place. Perspectivity is a fundamental characteristic of perception, because 'only God's conception is free of shadows' (Fink 1976: 203). Precisely because researchers are embodied perceivers, they can never take an absolutely objective standpoint, but can only conceive of the objects they experience within the limits of their embodied perception and understanding, i.e. against a specific (theoretical) background, in a specific context, and with a specific meaning. However, although researchers have a constitutive meaning for the mode in which the object they perceive appears, they must tolerate the knowledge that such objects also exist without their involvement.

With regard to the vignette, one might ask: Why is Sabine's physicality perceived and described, while that of other people in the vignette is not? Why do some people have names, while others remain anonymous? Why is clothing described for some and not for others? In the perception of the vignette writers, one thing acquires significance whereas another is disregarded. At the same time, the writers – with the help of a (research) group or PLC – consciously consider what finds its way into the vignette and what does not: the description of Sabine's physicality, for instance, can be read in contrast to the small, dark work of art. The anonymity of some of the people in the vignette illustrates Sabine's growing embeddedness in the work. The high heels have caught the attention of the vignette writer because of their loud noise. The loudness, which contrasts with the quietness of the museum, is unable to distract Sabine from her reflections. Much of this is revealed in atmospheres and moods that cannot easily be summed up in a single term. Vignettes are exemplifying, condensed descriptions that seek to express non-conceptual or non-propositional forms of experience (Bromand and Kreis 2010) such as those of being affected or touched (affiziert), and thus all that which largely eludes language. It is therefore helpful that in addition to what is said, vignette researchers also record the how of a speech act: Tone of voice, tempo, rhythm, facial expressions, gestures, posture, gait, clothing and body adornment find their way into the vignette and thus allow atmospheres and moods to be presented. Actual events are described as they are visibly embodied through bodily articulations in temporal and spatial contexts in the intersubjective perception and experience of the vignette writers. Time, for example, can fly by or drag on. It is precisely this relatively perceived experience of time that finds its way into the vignette. Both the collection and the evaluation of data are understood as selections that follow the criteria of aesthetic conciseness and sensuous experience. The aim is to visualize what is perceived in a concise way (in the sense of being pregnant-with-meaning) rather than to reconstruct the whole scene precisely and completely.

In writing or reading vignettes, researchers thus do not look at the world from the outside. They do not give things a meaning that is independent of them. What they write bears witness to their engagement with and involvement in the world. As such, vignettes have the potential to provide researchers with insights into the sensory contexts of specific experiential circumstances that would not be visible from the so-called objective perspective. That is, vignettes enable researchers to visualize what is revealed to them and how it is revealed. In doing so, vignettes represent an aesthetic experience of the world. Vignettes are a medium of sensuous and aesthetic visualization, and thus open up new spaces of cognition and interrelationship (Agostini 2017).

Intersubjectivity of research

Vignette 8: 'Karin and Mr Klotz'

For a project, Karin is supposed to play a piece on her accordion at the beginning of the English lesson. Before she starts playing, Mr Klotz asks her in a sharp tone: 'How many parts does the piece have?' Karin, loosening her grip on the accordion she has already taken hold of, answers shyly, 'Three.' – 'What are they called?' Karin, looking down: 'A – B – C.' Mr Klotz looks at her sternly, 'What do you call that?' Karin doesn't look up, her grip on the accordion tightens again, she doesn't answer. – 'It's called a trio!' Karin nods, then slips in a soft whispered 'yes'. Mr Klotz, instructing her to play, lifts his chin slightly. Karin bites her lips and begins to play, concentrating intently; she finishes the piece with a serious look on her face. After the last note, Mr Klotz says curtly, 'Yes. And look a little angrier when you play.' Without transition, he turns back to the class again: 'Take out your note books . . .' Karin puts the accordion away. Slightly flushed and clasping her hands, she says half aloud: 'Now I've embarrassed myself.'

AGOSTINI 2016b: 137

Did you feel anything when you read the vignette? Pity, discomfort, approval, disapproval? Did you think while reading or did you rather let yourself be drawn into the action? How do you experience Karin's experience? How does the teacher appear to you? Scenes like the one described in Vignette 8 are usually familiar to readers from their own (school) experiences. Feeling ashamed is a basic experience of human existence that can be shared by a lot of people. Phrases like 'blush with shame', 'want to sink into the ground with shame' or 'have one's eyes cast down in shame' describe these painful everyday experiences very tangibly in terms of one's own body. Trust and security in the world, but also in oneself, decrease. Experiences of shame go hand in hand with a loss of self-esteem: as a result, humans are strongly tied to their own visibility and want to hide it from others. The emotion of shame is regarded in a very particular way and indicates the tragic fate and normative social interactions in which a shamed person is fixed with the disciplining gaze of the other, perceived as a certain kind of person and thus is temporarily deprived of all further possibilities of knowing themself (Sartre 1980). 'Now I've embarrassed myself', seems to be Karin's admission of her own guilt, testifying to a lack of reflexive relationship with herself. Thus shame is the feeling of being, in the end, what Karin is for the other: She is held in the gaze of the (generalized) other and she is ashamed before the others (ibid.). It seems all the more serious when a student is intentionally shamed by and in front of others, as in the classroom scene described, and teachers like Mr Klotz reveal themselves less as educators, and more – due to strategic acts of shaming – as exercisers of power (Agostini 2016b; Agostini 2019).

Humans are embodied perceivers and are thus sensitive to bodily articulations such as gestures, facial expressions and manners of speaking, as you perhaps felt in your own body when reading the vignette at the beginning of this section. As bodily beings, Karin and Mr Klotz are accessible to you as a reader in their bodily articulations. Let's focus on Karin in detail. Her body expresses itself and reveals it to her classmates and the teacher, but also to the vignette writer and you as the reader of the vignette as something intersubjective that is perceivable and made tangible through their particular perspective. Even though Karin seems to be trying to save face, her face betrays a different intention. Her whole body speaks, the stooped posture, the ever-tightening grip on the accordion, the bite on the lip, the look at the floor. The body and its speech elude rational control; she does not have everything under control.

> If I try to study love or hate purely from inner observation, I will find very little to describe: a few pangs, a few heart throbs – in short, trite agitations which do not reveal the essence of love or hate . . . We must reject the prejudice which makes 'inner realities' out of love, hate or anger, leaving them accessible to one single witness: the person who feels them. Anger, shame, hate and love are not psychic facts hidden at the bottom of another's consciousness: they are types of behavior or styles of conduct which are visible from the outside.
>
> MERLEAU-PONTY 1964: 52–3

This bodily articulation helps you as a reader to experience how Karin may feel. Whether Karin has really had the experience you are co-experiencing is beyond all of our knowledge. What is important, therefore, is not what Karin really feels and what is 'behind' her story, but what you can experience through the physical connection via the vignette in order to learn something about (pedagogical) situations, relationships, social interactions or feelings. For researchers, the methodological power of the vignette lies in the phenomenological status of example. As an example, the vignette does not express what one knows through argument or conceptual explanation, but, in an evocative manner, it lets one experience (see, hear, feel . . .) what one does not know (yet) (Van Manen 2016: 256). Hence, the vignette can make the singular knowable, i.e. it brings out the particular or singularity of a certain phenomenon or event while at the same time providing access to a general or universal meaning. It reconciles the duality of the particular and the universal, in the sense that 'the phenomenological example expresses the singular as universal' (Van Manen and Van Manen 2021: 19). Suppose that someone comes up with a definitive and final formulation of what it is like to feel ashamed. You already know that it is not possible to say directly and satisfactorily what this experience is, so it is necessary to present it by means of examples. At best you can give an example of the experience of feeling ashamed by using the example of Karin when she has to play a piece on her accordion at the beginning of the English lesson. Hence, vignettes try to make 'the meaning of a phenomenon or event knowable in a way that the conceptual and argumentative dimensions of the text cannot achieve' (Van Manen 2016: 257). What you learn intersubjectively and in a general/universal sense from the example, you can also transfer to other situations involving shame. That is the 'learning effect' that vignettes bring.

You can read the vignette in different ways; it is understood differently against the background of your own individual previous experiences, knowledge, habits of interpretation, implicit and explicit theoretical points of reference. Vignette readings – see section entitled 'Vignette reading' – are offers of meaning and understanding. Only because you can read the body language of others directly in an intersubjective sense are you able to write vignettes and understand them in multiple ways.

Hence, vignettes aim to exemplify and explore intersubjective experience. In line with the work of Meyer-Drawe (2001: 11), vignette writers assume that this includes the world of the in-between (*inter*), and thus that experiences between researchers and participants are also intersubjective. In this understanding it is only through these experiences that subjectivity or objectivity can subsequently be distinguished in the first place. The reference point for intersubjective perceptions and experiences is the body as the situation and reality of all experience. Thus, as with Merleau-Ponty (2009) and his concept of *intercorporéité* or *intercorporeality*, it becomes clear that you as the researcher need the alien 'other' to provide you with access to yourselves and thus to your own (bodily) experiences. The lived experiences of others elude you as a perceiver, but their bodily articulations do not. As a perceiver, you are always also affected by the bodily expressions of others. This means that, in a shared experience, others reveal something that you can also experience in your own body. In relation to the example of Karin and Mr Klotz, this means you can also experience the shame of Karin's experiences in your own body. You can read (and maybe also feel) the blush that spreads across her face as a blush of shame. Hence, vignette research is the right approach for those who seek to understand not only their own 'first-person' experiences, but also the first-person experiences of others. This 'second-person perspectivity' as a mode of resonating with the expressions of others can bring you as researcher closer to a lived understanding of what it means to be doing phenomenology close to the other. Second-person perspectivity happens, 'when I allow myself to resonate with the other: where I become the "second person" whom the other addresses' (Churchill 2012: 2). Scott Churchill reinforces this point: ' "Second-person perspectivity" is a special mode of access to the other that occurs within the first-person plural: in experiencing the other within the we, we are open to the other as a "thou", another "myself" – and, in this same moment, I become an intimate "Other" to the one with whom I find myself in an "exchange" ' (ibid.).

Based on the body schema developed by Merleau-Ponty (2009) in the context of intercorporeality, pre-predicative and pre-reflexive correspondence with the other is possible, i.e. the other's experience can be experienced before it has been addressed, named or reflected upon; and in this intercorporeal encounter, (new) meaning can emerge. Thus, in a shared experiential situation, intersubjective social meaning potentially arises and can be attributed neither to you alone nor to the other alone; however, the other is necessary to its expression.

Vignettes emerge from the co-experiential experience of vignette writers. Following Ton Beekman (1987), who coined the term 'participatory experience', vignette research traces co-experiential experience. Such a research stance assumes that, unlike behaviour, we cannot observe experience, but we can co-experientially experience others as experiencers (Laing 1967). In this sense, experiences can be shared, with researchers reporting their experiences of the experiences of those involved in an experiential situation. Thus, vignettes capture intersubjective moments of perception and experience by which researchers in the field are affected, or 'struck'. One can be struck when habitual courses of action or categories of understanding are thwarted, and a new meaning emerges. Vignettes are an attempt to set down this co-experiential experience in writing. Memorable moments are thus transformed into narrative text and, in the course of writing, the vignette writers themselves will have had experiences and undergone learning (Agostini 2017).

Vignettes do not claim to reconstruct situations or provide a full contextualization of them, instead they translate into language the actions, bodily expressions, atmospheres and moods that are significant aspects of experience in an aesthetically pregnant way. Moments of condensed experience are selected, and an attempt is made to preserve ambivalences and ambiguities in the description as far as possible. Vignettes thus describe what is stimulating, attractive or repulsive, what pre-empts preconceived expectations. They show how readers' experiences can lead them to understand the self, the world and others differently than they did before. Accordingly, vignette writers seek to pay attention to unexpected events that give rise to meaning by virtue of their ambiguity and, in consequence, make learning possible.

Phenomenological research is thus based on the intersubjective character of experience. For example, by reproducing the actions depicted in a vignette, readers can verify the plausibility of the concrete example for themselves. Hence, vignettes refer to intersubjective and therefore relational experiences, which can be intuitively understood and therefore recognized by their readers. It is only this comprehensibility that gives validity to a vignette. This communicative validation process (we also refer to it as 'resonance reading', see section entitled 'Resonance reading'; for 'resonance', please see section entitled 'Accessing the fragility of human action') is undertaken in a (research) group: in a PLC or a community of practice. In a group discussion of vignettes, the limits and potentialities of linguistically condensed experiences are co-reflected upon and the practices of looking and interpreting are made transparent. Thus, the creation of the text and the condensation of the vignette text pose challenges for writers on several levels. The ongoing writing work and the discussion of it within groups can reveal the writer's own blind spots and linguistic inaccuracies in relation to what he/she intended to depict.

The writing of vignettes starts with the methodological research processes of bracketing and phenomenological reduction. In the phenomenological setting, the difference between 'content' and 'mode of access', or between 'thing' and 'meaning', is brought into view and 'what is shown is reduced to the way it is shown' (Waldenfels 1992: 15). According to Michael Schratz, Johanna F. Schwarz and Tanja Westfall-Greiter (2012: 35), '[t]he vignette does not describe, it does not assert, it shows'. On the one hand, vignettes require a reflexive consideration of which pre-reflexive, linguistic means should be used in order to retain the concreteness of experiences and to avoid the danger of linguistically abstract and intellectual generalizations, which prompt a hasty switch to a meta-level, leaving the lifeworld of the persons described behind. On the other hand, it is important to clarify which details of the situation are brought to bear in the overall composition and which are not. To a certain extent, these requirements represent a technical and learnable side of phenomenological (writing) work. Thus, contextual information flows into the vignette only insofar as it appears as important and offers readers relevant cues within the vignette's approach to understanding. The moments of experience thus framed become universal in a certain sense, pointing beyond the particular context, and yet they are clearly recognizable as concrete moments of experience. Contextual proximity is also ensured in the use of actual statements recorded both in transcripts and in conversations. Stronger contextualization is undertaken in the vignette readings (see 'Vignette reading' section).

Starting from the raw material, any exact and detailed description of the complete situation is dispensed with, since a complete contextualization would risk providing causal explanations of what is revealed in the vignette, and potentially lead to objectification. In order to be able to capture the atmosphere of the scene, writers and groups must always weigh up what degree of detail to aim for, to ensure that it does not detract from the conciseness of the description. Putting together experiences based on different actions, the vignette makes material both what researchers have participated in and what they have not. Experiential protocols frame the setting in terms of the focus of the gaze as well as of the researchers' experiences. The specific composition and presentation of a vignette directs readers' perceptual focus towards a particular selection of experiences. The meanings of what is perceived are already co-constituted through linguistic condensation. On the one hand, such condensed descriptions of experiences refer to pre-reflexive access to the world; on the other hand, the transformation of the scene into language, with its associated aestheticization and reflection on meaning, means vignettes contain reflexive elements, but also surpluses of meaning that are immanent to the text, allowing connotations to be released through association (Gabriel 2010: 375).

Ethical standards and research responsibilities

Ethical questions and guidelines are of relevance for vignette research, as they are for all empirical – quantitative and qualitative – research. Beyond the actual research goal, the well-being of all those involved in the process must therefore be kept in mind, and research relationships should be subjected to regulation. In this sense, ethical considerations have to permeate all phases of the research process – from planning to analysis to completion – and have to be reflected in all phases of research. Ethical research requirements require, for example, appropriate preliminary clarifications, agreements, participant declarations of consent and respectful handling of the data collected. Different ethics codes provide specific standards to cover most situations encountered by researchers across a range of disciplines. Their goals are the welfare and protection of the individuals and groups to whom they apply and the education of institution members, students, and the public regarding disciplines' ethical standards:

> The development of a dynamic set of ethical standards ... requires a personal commitment and lifelong effort to act ethically; to encourage ethical behavior by students, supervisees, employees, and colleagues; and to consult with others concerning ethical problems.
>
> APA 2017: 3

According to the ethical guidelines of the American Psychological Association (APA 2017: 3–4), research processes must attach great importance to the fundamental principles of 'Beneficence and Nonmaleficence', 'Fidelity and Responsibility', 'Integrity', 'Justice' and 'Respect for People's Rights and Dignity' throughout. All participants in studies must be respected and their basic human rights must be protected. In addition, efforts must be made to ensure the well-being and safety of the individuals participating in the research as far as possible, to treat them with respect in accordance with ethical principles, and to recognize their competence and reliability as participants (ibid.). Researchers' entry into the research field brings with it the need for an appreciative perception of the (institutional) culture in question and the adoption of a responsive attitude (see the 'Responsivity as a virtue' section). Vignette research must take into consideration the specific organizational conditions in the field. A tactful approach to individuals and situations is an important prerequisite for participation in the research process.

Informed consent is only deemed to have been given when personal data is collected with the consent of participants who have been adequately informed about the purpose, conditions and effects of their participation in the research process, that is, only once participants are fully informed about the research project can their verbal and written consent be obtained for the study and for the recording of the data (APA 2017: 10–11). Furthermore, special reference must be made to the voluntary nature of participation, i.e. participants' ability to cease to participate in the research at any time or to subsequently withdraw information that has already been given (ibid.: 13). This aspect is of particular relevance for vignette research, as co-experiential experience can lead to observations that the participants may not want to see written down. Furthermore, participants have to be informed in advance about the duration and content of the field visits. In addition, individuals participating in the study must be assured of respect, confidentiality and anonymity with regard to the results (ibid.: 11; see also Allen 2017). Thus, all persons depicted in vignettes are anonymised, and the exact contexts are described in such a way that vignettes cannot be traced back to specific places or circumstances. The principle of co-experiential experience in particular requires discussion of participants' personal experiences in the course of the study, in order to uncover possible negative effects. In order to write vignettes, researchers allow themselves to be struck by what happens in the field and what they perceive through their senses: this is intersubjective, co-experiential experience.

The particular challenge of writing vignettes is to take into account the mood of a situation and influences that cannot be expressed in words, i.e., to take a linguistic approach to something that cannot easily be expressed in language. Attention is, therefore, paid in particular to bodily expression, and the focus is not solely on verbal expression and cognitive performance. In the mode of co-experiential experiencing, people or habits can come into view who/ that were not intended be perceived or observed. The same can happen with experiences that are perceived but are embarrassing or shameful for the perceived person. The body always reveals more than it would like to reveal, e.g. in the case of embarrassment through red cheeks. In reading the vignette, you can also experience an individual as someone that they do not actually want to be. Vignettes should therefore be discussed gently with participants, taking into account their sensations and feelings. In addition, participants should be provided with a contact and encouraged to get in touch if they have any questions, uncertainties or doubts. They should also feel able to raise any questions they may have both before and during the study.

The publishing of vignettes raises the question of data accuracy and ownership. According to APA (2017: 12) researchers '[should] not present portions of another's work or data as their own, even if the other work or data source is cited occasionally'. Hence, research data should be neither falsified nor invented, and one's own and others' contributions must be clearly presented (APA 2017: 12). With regard to vignettes, this also means that the source where the vignette was first published must be indicated. Depending on the arrangements within a research group, the author or authors' name(s) (for example in the case of joint authorship) must also be given.

Online research also poses a particular challenge, not only in terms of obtaining consent (e.g. being allowed to record sessions), but also in terms of the research process and the safeguarding of quality criteria.

Vignette 9: 'Teacher education and Agenda 2030'

> In the German-language parallel breakaway session on the future contribution of teacher education programmes to the 2030 Agenda, the facilitator Ulrike, the researcher Manuela, and the student Mina, are already present ten minutes before the official start time. The researcher-observer thanks her student Mina for coming and wants to know how her newborn child is doing. Mina explains happily that the little boy is doing well. Punctually at 12.00 pm, Ulrike opens her PowerPoint presentation and says in a calm tone of voice, addressing those present, 'We are now looking at gender justice again'. Two more people, Anna, a young blonde woman, and Lucas, a man with greying hair, join the

session a little late. There are now eight people in the virtual room, and they briefly introduce themselves and their areas of work. They all have their cameras switched on and are clearly visible and audible next to the presentation on the screen. Ulrike calmly introduces the topic with her first question: 'How would you define Goal 5? What do you understand by it?' Time passes, no one answers. A little restless, Ulrike speaks up again and tells the participants they can speak freely. Now Anna clears her throat, introduces herself briefly, then the words burst out of her as she laughs and shakes her head: 'I'm sorry I'm late, I've just had a baby with me, we've just had a few problems.' She gives a short laugh, then continues laughing, 'I'm afraid I'll have to take a bit of a sho ... leave again in a while.' Anna pauses briefly before starting to answer the question. The participants smile understandingly into their cameras.

ELOFF et al. 2023: 623–4[2]

How is it possible for researchers to access co-experiential experience if they are not even in the same room as the participants? We faced this particular challenge in a project on the Sustainable Development Goals (SDGs) in teacher education (Eloff et al. 2022), where we had to collect vignettes online in a series of webinars. When writing vignettes online, one risks losing sight of experience and research as a responsive event in which all participants can gain knowledge about themselves, the other and the world through their physical corporeality. Some participants turned off their cameras and muted their microphones. Hence, the glances between participants were no longer met, different remarks were not responded to, sounds took on a different tone or faded away, and experiences were not perceived. Nevertheless, experiences do occur in online settings and can be brought into focus with the help of vignettes that make participants' bodily articulations perceptible. The best possible technological conditions are needed to make this possible, but so is a particular sensitivity on the part of researchers: a sensitivity that is able to perceive intermediate tones or discords and to express perceived inadequacies.

Phenomenological research is embedded in the lifeworld of researchers and participants, but at the same time it is assessed on the basis of its ability to suspend personal or systemic bias, its originality of insight, and its scholarly treatment of sources (Van

Manen 2016: 347). However, traditional measures or quality criteria such as content validity, criterion-related validity and construct validity are more relevant for tests and measures and are not compatible with phenomenological vignettes.

Quality criteria in qualitative research

A common problem for vignette researchers is the challenge to define their study with reference to approaches that do not belong to the methodology of descriptive phenomenology. The application of concepts of validation, such as sample size, sampling selection criteria, member checking and empirical generalization is especially problematic for phenomenological vignettes. These are concepts that belong to the languages of different methodologies and cannot be uncritically applied to vignette research. However, it is methodologically and ethically commendable that vignettes derived from experiential protocols are resonant with their original experience. Experiential protocols provide an intersubjectively comprehensible basis for vignette research. They also serve to increase the plausibility of vignettes; they recall the experienced events step by step and have the status of evidence. In experiential protocols, researchers record direct speech, conspicuities and questions as well as their own thoughts, impressions and feelings, with the aim of documenting and critically reflecting on their resonance for the research process. Resonance questions can include:

1 What is my response to the results of the field phase?
2 What were my expectations and fears before the field phase?
3 Which expectations and fears were confirmed? Which were not?
4 To what extent did I deviate from the agreed instruments/ procedure? Why?
5 Which findings did I (not) report back and why?
6 What do I want to change in the next phase?

Phenomenological validation of the quality of experiential accounts is a means of comprehending the actions depicted in the vignettes, allowing researchers to verify the plausibility of the example for themselves. The validity of a vignette lies in its comprehensibility (Lippitz 1987: 117). Behind this is the attempt to give a vignette the greatest possible credibility by means of intersubjective validation or communication, for example in the form of resonance reading (see 'Presenting your raw vignette' and 'Resonance reading' sections). Another criterion is whether the phenomenological themes emerging from the descriptions are appropriate and original and whether the phenomenological analysis is executed in a scholarly manner. But what validation criteria are appropriate when reviewing phenomenological vignettes? Questions 1–7 may be considered with regard to a vignette and addressed to a vignette reading to test its level of validity (Agostini et al. 2023a: 42):

Vignette:

1 Perspective on perception(s)/experience(s): Is/are the perception(s)/experience(s) described in a relatable way, as co-experiential experience, so that readers are literally drawn into the vignette? Does the vignette retain its ambiguousness? Does it include terms that suggest an unambiguous interpretation and that could work against the intended ambiguity of a vignette?

2 Condensed language: Is the vignette focused on description? Does it divide pre-reflexive, reflexive, precise and concise elements in such a way as to describe emotional and physical aspects in a tangible, vivid and concise manner? Does it succeed in avoiding any explanatory meta-perspective or condensed interpretation?

3 Knowledge: Does the vignette serve as an exemplification? Is the depiction of the vignette formulated so as to enable readers to draw a general lesson or broader knowledge from the specific case in question? Can readers learn something new from the vignette? Does the vignette 'disrupt' familiar situations and assumptions?

Vignette reading:

4 Focus: Are the focus of the analysis and the affective moment made clear and comprehensible in the vignette

reading? Is there a phenomenological approach that elaborates 'something-as-something' and a focus on the theme of the vignette?

5 Pointing and theory reference: Is there a 'pointing to' instead of a 'pointing out'? Is there an insertion of meaning, e.g. on the basis of theoretical references? Are potential meanings described beyond the moment of perception or experience described? Are the ambiguities in the vignette also retained in the vignette reading?

6 Knowledge: Are general/universal elements in the specific perceptual experience pointed out? Is the (future) knowledge value made clear?

General conduct of the phenomenological study:

7 Is the researcher/author aware of the method and methodology and their implications (e.g. do they make clear their own point of view, limits of experience)? Is this reflexivity evident (in-)directly in the vignette as well as in the vignette reading?

Phenomenological evidence has to do with grasping the meaning of a phenomenon or event. However, phenomenological evidence is ambiguous and never complete. Therefore Merleau-Ponty, as an body phenomenologist, criticized Husserl's claim that the intentionality of a phenomenon can be grasped through eidetic reduction (see section entitled 'Related approaches'). With vignettes, evidence is meaning-based and focuses on understanding the pre-reflexive dimensions of the lifeworlds depicted. Furthermore, phenomenology is an approach that does not yield generalizations in the usual empirical sense. However, according to Van Manen (2016: 352), 'we could speak of phenomenological understandings as generalized'.

So we could ask, how is phenomenological generalization possible while respecting singularity and uniqueness? For example, how can we keep a focus on the singularity of the phenomenon while still being able to arrive at some type of universal or generalized insight into this phenomenon?

Ibid.

According to Van Manen, there are two kinds of phenomenological generalizations: existential and singular. The first is focused on eidetic or essential understanding and asks what is universal or essential about a phenomenon in an existential sense. This form of generalization makes it possible to recognize recurring aspects of the meaning of a certain phenomenon. The second generalization is focused on what is singular or unique (ibid.). Phenomenological vignettes fall into this second area. As examples, vignettes are considered singular generalizations that make it possible to recognize what is universal about a phenomenon.

PART TWO

Doing Vignette Research

CHAPTER THREE

Starting the Research and Writing Vignettes

This chapter describes the step-by-step process that can serve as a rough guide for the comprehensive process of creating, crafting and presenting vignettes. The process of writing vignettes is organic and unique to each vignette researcher. There is a 'rhythm' and a process which is, to a great extent, determined by the personal preferences and unique strengths of the individual vignette researcher, while also being guided by the characteristics of a vignette. The 'stepwise' process described here therefore represents a broad guideline for the comprehensive process of creating, crafting and presenting vignettes. It can be interpreted flexibly and adapted to your specific research contexts.

Preparation for vignettes

Before embarking on the journey of collecting data for vignette writing, several preceding processes are needed. In the same way that a research focus needs to be articulated, vignette writing also requires the focus of the vignettes to be explicitly articulated. Yet, at the same time, vignette research requires an openness on the part of the researcher, an ongoing receptivity to the ways in which phenomena may be present in the field. In addition, the vignette researcher also needs to be aware of paradigmatic and theoretical assumptions that will inadvertently infuse the vignettes (see 'Accessing the fragility of human action', 'Responsivity as a virtue', 'Vignettes as a transformative force', and 'The phenomenological attitude' sections).

Articulating the focus for the vignette

Even though the provenance of vignette research, as articulated by the IVR group, was educational sciences, vignette research is applicable to a variety of disciplines. It can be conducted anywhere in the observable, experiential world and it aligns with a multitude of narrative research inquiries (Clandinin 2006, 2019; Miles 1990) in various fields of research (see Table 1 in the 'Related approaches' section). Some vignette researchers articulate a clear focus prior to data collection, while others prefer to enter the research field by being open to the ways in which phenomena may be present in the field. There is no 'right' or 'wrong' way to find a research focus in vignette research. Articulating a broad focus prior to data collection may provide parameters for researchers within which phenomena can be explored. On the other hand, approaching the research by being 'open' to the experience may, in turn, offer unanticipated insights.

There are therefore diverse experiential layers in the articulation of a focus for vignette research. It can, for instance, be defined very broadly in terms of the educational, psychological, sociological, sociopolitical, behavioural, cognitive or affective dimensions. For example, a vignette may focus on classroom management, the psychological dynamics of disrupted learning, the status of teachers, the behaviours of school principals, the cognitive patterns of language learning or the experience of affection between young children. Vignettes can also be defined at a more granular and phenomenon-specific level. They may consider specific aspects of teaching and learning, or the details of high-level political negotiations. They can zoom in on the behaviour of health professionals during times of crisis, the manifestations of gender identity in climate change discussions, or the brush strokes of an artist in the Arctic Circle. By way of example: a vignette researcher has the option to start with a very wide lens by studying 'psychology'. But the researcher can also refine this, focusing on positive psychology, or even further by studying well-being, or one aspect of well-being such as the phenomenon of relationships. A vignette researcher can also study one relationship between two people, or one aspect of one relationship between two people or even one single moment in which one aspect of one relationship between two people is experienced. The notion of finding a focus for a vignette is therefore flexible in and of itself, but it has to be related to the co-experiential experience that is reported and subsequently to the experiential protocol, so it is not merely random. Phenomena can be present at a more systemic level (e.g. psychology), and studied accordingly, but they can also be present within the minutiae of a broad phenomenon (e.g. a singular moment depicting the psychological relationship between two people).

This flexibility within vignette research to set the level of magnification of the study provides an important vehicle for knowledge creation. It is the prerogative of the vignette researcher not only to determine the focus of the study, but also to determine the ratio at which the focal length of the phenomenon is co-experientially experienced. Returning to the inherent flexibility of vignette research, it should be noted that valuable insights might also be garnered from vignette studies that deliberately choose not to articulate a focus. This might capture unanticipated experiences and phenomena and contribute to knowledge development in a specific field. For instance, a market researcher may enter a health food store with an 'open mind' and not have a predetermined focus for gathering data. This may afford the researcher insights into the ways in which customer experiences could be enhanced, how product placement affects customer behaviours or how check-out processes could be made more efficient. Even though this 'open approach' might necessitate flexibility on the part of the vignette researcher, new (and valuable) knowledge may nevertheless be generated.

Remaining open to the experience

It is critical for vignette researchers to remain open to the experience of the phenomenon under study. In its essence, vignette research considers co-experiential experiences with the goal of presenting the experiences of others in a format that can reduce the distance between the researcher and the researched. For the process of co-experiential experiences to be optimally captured, vignette researchers need to enter, remain in, and exit the research setting with an open mind, and perhaps in some ways an 'open heart' as well. This is compellingly argued by Meyer-Drawe (2017: 14), who states: 'Phenomenology as a philosophy of experience means the attempt to understand the experiences of the world, the other and of myself, even if there is an inevitable distance between my concrete, situated experiences and my return to them while I am talking or thinking about them.' In terms of remaining 'open to the experience', a good 'exercise' as a vignette researcher, in practical terms, would be to constantly ask yourself questions: What is happening here? What must it be like for this person, here in this situation? How does it feel? What is this making me think of? What am I seeing/hearing/smelling/feeling/thinking in this moment?

Awareness of theoretical assumptions

Vignette researchers bring their own personal life, educational and professional experiences to the study of phenomena. In studying phenomena and capturing experiences, the theoretical assumptions of vignette researchers may therefore affect the initial data that is captured to craft the vignettes, and as such also the final vignettes. A vignette researcher with a background in inclusive education may for instance note the children with disabilities in a classroom more distinctly, or a researcher with a background in mathematics may be specifically interested in how children engage with numerical problem-solving activities. Awareness of personal theoretical assumptions is therefore critical. Some vignette researchers write reflective notes to make their own assumptions visible prior to the vignette study. Others engage in group discussions afterwards to elucidate the intricacies of theoretical assumptions that may be informing the vignette process. It may even be that a vignette researcher only becomes aware of theoretical assumptions during the group discussions or resonance readings (see 'Presenting your raw vignette' and 'Resonance reading' sections). If a phenomenon is captured too interpretatively in the vignette, the group may assist the vignette researcher to craft the text to reflect the way the phenomenon appeared initially. In a similar way to theoretical assumptions, vignette researchers' personal experiences may also influence the kind of vignettes they choose. If a vignette researcher, for instance, was slightly rebellious in formal educational settings, he or she may be particularly intrigued by children exhibiting similar behaviours in a classroom. These pre-assumptions are an inevitability in all research. As with other research methodologies, explicit awareness of such pre-assumptions is therefore critical.

Sampling and participants

As phenomenological researchers, vignette researchers seek to find 'what is singular' (Van Manen 2016: 353). Vignette research does not necessarily seek similarities or patterns or even 'information-rich' participants. Rather, the participants in vignette research are inadvertently selected by the gaze and directed attention of the vignette researcher. This leaves room for uniqueness to emerge. How many vignettes should I write? How many participants should I observe? These are questions that are often asked by novice vignette researchers. In the same way that Van Manen (2016: 353) cautions within the broad phenomenological research domain that 'too many transcripts may ironically encourage shallow reflection', vignette researchers predominantly prioritize depth within the co-experiential experience, in preference to large samples of participants.

Finding your setting

Vignette research can be conducted in any environment. For vignette researchers, it helps to articulate where this environment would be for a specific study. Will it be taking place indoors or outdoors, or in a public or a private space? In educational research, will the environment be a place of formal or informal learning, in a school or in a specific classroom? Other social scientists may use home or work environments, and for yet other vignette researchers the setting may be somewhere sports or cultural activities take place. For natural scientists, vignette research settings may include laboratories, archaeological sites, hospitals, clinics, construction sites, forests, and the ocean, rivers, lakes, mountains or the Sahara

Desert. Vignette research may be conducted on trains, ships, airplanes, tunnels, bridges or in a small corner of a large factory. It will be determined by the curiosity of the vignette researcher and the infinite possibilities offered by accessing those research settings. The potency of vignettes to engage participants across a variety of research settings has been persuasively argued (Heldbjerg and Van Liempd 2018).

Considering the spaces and places where vignette research will be carried out is an important preparatory step for vignette researchers. In some instances, ethical clearance may need to be obtained to gain entrance to the setting. For instance, due to health regulations or protocols, prior permission may be needed at certain sites, as well as consent from the participants within the setting. As explained in the 'Ethical standards and research responsibilities' section, the ethics protocols for good research practices should also be in place for vignette researchers. In terms of finding a specific setting for the vignette research though, these factors need to be considered ahead of time. Box 2 presents some questions that the vignette researcher may utilize to capture settings.

Box 2 Capturing settings

Who is present?
Where is it?
When is it?
What is happening?
How is it happening/presenting?

In addition to physical environments, vignette research has also increasingly been conducted in online environments (Eloff et al. 2022). In these instances, the 'research setting' may entail online group discussions, webinars, online lectures, conference participation or formal meetings. For the vignette researcher, the crafting of vignettes in an online environment may present unique challenges (see section entitled 'Quality criteria in qualitative research'). Vignette researchers seek to portray the embodied experiences of others within vignettes. In an online environment, however, vignette researchers need to deal with increased anonymity and a reduced ability to assess non-verbal communication. In addition, the use of technology and the variety of online platforms present another layer of challenges when the vignette researcher seeks to access the experience of the other (e.g. co-experiential experience). For instance, the vignette researcher may experience connectivity challenges, while the participant whose experiences are being captured may not be experiencing challenges.

As with other research settings, the practical implications for the vignette researcher may thus need to be considered beforehand. This may relate to ensuring good connectivity, gaining consent from participants, deciding about the use of recordings and defining the role of the vignette researcher explicitly (Boon 2021). Online meetings are often recorded, whereas the co-experiential experiences captured by vignette researchers are usually through observations via their senses. In instances where recordings have been made (and the necessary permissions have been granted), the vignette researcher may have an additional resource, being able to return to the recording after the fact in order to check aspects of the context and the specifics of direct speech. However, it should be noted that checking a recording is not a replacement for capturing the experience itself, due to the time/space difference that would be present. Vignettes capture experiences *in situ*, and recordings would therefore only serve a supplementary purpose, rather than acting as a substitute for the experience itself.

Experiential protocols: noting your observations and perceptions

What captures your attention?

This is the question that drives the observations/perceptions of a vignette researcher and the experiential protocols that he or she creates from them. The German word *Anspruch* infuses many of the early writings of the IVR group (Schratz, Schwarz and Westfall-Greiter 2012; Schratz, Schwarz and Westfall-Greiter 2013; Schwarz 2012), because an early methodological decision was to 'follow where your own attention goes' as a vignette researcher. The direct

English translation of this word (*Anspruch*), for instance, is given as 'irritation', but the concept that underpins *Anspruch* is actually much richer, and deeper, than mere 'irritation'. Most importantly, *Anspruch* can hold both positive and negative connotations. It is about 'capturing' attention. For the vignette researcher, the translations 'appealing', 'claiming', 'attracting' should therefore be considered in terms of the phenomenon towards which attention is directed. It is about what 'draws you in' as you co-experientially experience the dynamics of a research setting. More crystallized translations of the word *Anspruch* would therefore also include words such as 'provocation', 'challenge', 'stimulation', 'excitement', 'suggestion', 'causation', 'appealing' and even 'tickle'. What piques your interest? What intrigues you? What do you notice? What do you stumble upon? What do you find confusing? In English, these questions could potentially be questions for a vignette researcher to guide the ways in which attention unfolds. The gaze of the vignette researcher facilitates the content of the observations and perceptions, and ultimately the final vignette.

Drafting experiential protocols and noting observations and perceptions in vignette research is therefore much more than writing an objective, almost clinical account of a research setting. It is about following the path of your own interest and paying attention to the nuances, the pathos and the emotive dimensions of the phenomenon you are investigating. The physical environment does form part of the observation notes in the experiential protocols of vignette research, but it is just one aspect of them. In many ways the notes on the physical environment inform the dynamic dimensions of the phenomenon under study. The vignette researcher co-experientially experiences the physical environment, thereby instigating the perceptual resonance with the participant/s.

The practical aspects of writing vignette observations and perceptions should also be considered. After a setting for the study has been identified and access has been obtained, it is also important to determine the dates and times on/at which the co-experiential experience will be captured. The raw notes of a vignette researcher often start with the date and time, the place of research and notes on who is present in the research setting. It may be helpful to make a small sketch to capture these details. The time of the day, the time of the year, and seasonal changes may all affect the nature of co-experiential experiences. By paying attention to these kinds of details, the vignette researcher enriches the depth of the study.

Some vignette researchers prefer to capture their experiential protocols in notebooks, using a pen or pencil. Other vignette researchers prefer to use electronic devices with folders for the various sets of co-experiential experiences that they capture across different studies. There is a wide scope for the personal preference of vignette researchers in this regard. The most important thing is that the notes should be as detailed as possible. Often the notes of a vignette researcher are not perfect in terms of word use – they may even include abbreviations – but are rich in terms of the way they capture all the various dimensions of the phenomenon at a specific moment and as a specific scene.

The experiential protocols of vignette researchers are exceptionally detailed. They capture sights and sounds and smells and atmosphere, and perceive colours, light and shadows, acoustics and the changes within each of these sensory experiences. The observations/perceptions of vignette researchers thus habitually depict a physical environment in minute detail. Notes often report on the clothing, hairstyles, eye colours, footwear or accessories of participants. They frequently describe the dimensions of a room, the style of the windows and doors or the type of flooring. They could include descriptions of furniture, lighting, temperature, the colour of the curtains or the way the sun shines through a window. Vignette researchers report on language use, gestures, facial expressions, intonation, mimicry and even the quality of a voice in a room. The purpose of these details is to illustrate the co-experiential experience. Box 3 presents some questions that may be used to capture sensory observations.

Box 3 Capturing sensory observations

What do I see?
What do I hear?
What do I smell?
What am I tasting?
Which textures am I touching?

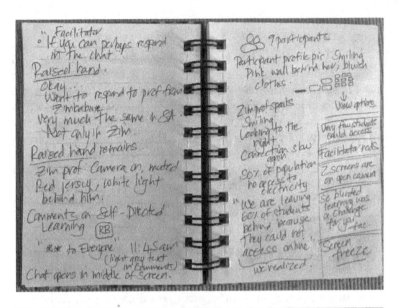

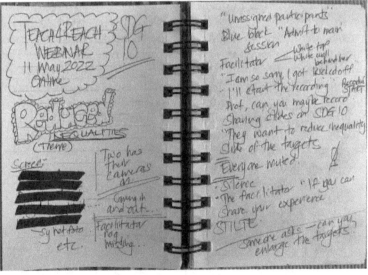

FIGURES 3 and 4 *Examples of experiential protocols by a vignette researcher.*
Source: Authors

Vignette researchers may also explore phenomena on numerous levels, e.g. historically, linguistically, aesthetically, psychologically or educationally. As such, the interactions between research participants and the environments in which they live are captured by the vignette researcher in a way that will inform the research, but which also will enable a co-experiential experience (see 'Accessing the fragility of human action' and 'The phenomenological attitude' sections). In creating this co-experiential experience, it is the prerogative of the vignette researcher to foreground specific dimensions of the experience, and within this process of capturing perceptions, this 'foregrounding' will be highly dependent on the openness of the vignette researcher to the phenomenon itself and the essence of the experience. In addition, the vignette researcher needs to show high receptivity to the emotive dimensions of the experience. Vignette researchers are thus often advised to experience the phenomena as 'a full human being' and to constantly be asking questions. What is this experience doing to me? How am I experiencing this at this moment? How is this phenomenon showing itself to me? What does it show? A critical next step, however, would be to translate it as a co-experiential experience, turning the personal, embodied experience into a pathic description of the experience of another. Box 4 presents some questions that may be used to capture behaviour and actions.

Box 4 Capturing behaviour and actions

What actions do I perceive?
What is being done?
What movement can be detected?
What are the facial expressions I perceive?

In order to fully capture this human experience, some vignette researchers also use drawings in conjunction with their written experiential protocols. For example, they might draw the positions of people around a table or the facial expressions of participants as they are speaking. They may include pictures of how they are feeling themselves. Drawings are valuable tools for vignette researchers when they start the process of writing raw vignettes. They can save time while they are in the field, but they can also capture aspects of an experience that might not be easily expressed in words in the moment. In conjunction with drawings, vignette researchers may also use abbreviations and acronyms to optimize their note-taking. They may use well-known acronyms, but they may also develop personal acronyms that work well for them.

Great caution is advisable with regard to the use of photographs for data collection during vignette research. Some vignette researchers do take photographs in order to capture the details of a specific setting or an artefact. However, other vignette researchers have indicated that photographing presents numerous complexities in terms of the efficacy with which experiences are captured. They argue firstly, that taking photographs is an experience in and of itself and perhaps distinct from the experience of 'being in the moment'. Secondly, they point out that individuals' behaviours tend to change with the awareness of a camera, and the fact that photographs are being taken thereby inadvertently affects the experiences that are being captured for the vignette study. Thirdly, the idea that vignettes are 'pregnant' with the potential that is communicated through the description of 'what might be', may be diminished by the use of photographs. Photographs tend to capture 'what is', rather than what is invisible to the eye. Vignette researchers who do use photographs in turn point out that photographs may assist the vignette researcher to enhance the precision of their descriptions and may serve as a memory bank for their experiences. They also indicate that they may take photographs before they start to craft experiential protocols, thereby leaving the observation phase of the study free from the interruption of picture-taking. The general consensus, therefore, is that photographs can be taken during vignette research, but only used as a minor supplementary tool. When they are taken, they should be used with much care and sensitivity. Pictures should not be taken of the participants themselves, unless explicit consent (and assent in the case of children) has been given.

A vignette researcher should preferably have a singular focus during the period of the co-experiential experience. For social science researchers, this may mean a very specific focus on one individual, one interaction or one situation. While it may be tempting to have multiple foci during the process of data collection (e.g. observations and fieldwork), it is the intention of vignette researchers to capture data at the personal level. As such, vignettes usually depict the experience of one, two or only a few persons. There is often also only one central figure in the vignette. There might be several other players, but the vignette researcher predominantly seeks to portray the experience of one person or one phenomenon, and the 'others' in the vignette frequently serve to inform the experience of a more central figure. This singular focus does not, however, mean that the minutiae of 'others' are not captured in equal detail. It is often within the minutiae that the poignancy of the vignette resides. Thus, by describing the minute details of others in the vignette, the vignette researcher may be communicating the co-experiential experience more personally, and in more depth.

The languages of vignettes

Usually, vignette researchers write observation/perception notes in their first language for reasons of expediency. Capturing observation data in a first language creates a proximity within the experience and also potentially allows for more details to be captured, because the vignette researcher does not need to spend time on translation (Eloff 2021). These notes may be translated into other languages later, or translation may take place during the writing of the raw vignettes. Some vignette researchers have indicated that 'translation processes are also helpful in extracting the conciseness of a vignette, leaving out the superfluous and carefully considering every word chosen' (Agostini 2022: 1).

Accessing the lifeworlds of participants should ideally present a continuous challenge for researchers. In this regard, the language dynamic in vignette research is of interest. Vignette research presents opportunities to increase the understanding of a wide variety of complex phenomena, including phenomena that are rooted in linguistic lifeworlds. The language landscapes of the vignette researcher may be homogeneous, but are more likely multilingual. This means there may be several sets of linguistic dynamics at play during data collection. In a monolingual setting, capturing data in participants' first language may, for instance, provide miniscule insights that may ultimately lead to extensive new systems of knowledge. Similarly, capturing data in the vignette researcher's first language may create deeply nuanced layers, as the researcher seeks to translate the exactness of the experiences. In turn, capturing data multilingually may mean that invisible nuances are captured (or lost), and that the pause that is needed for the purpose of translation adds depth to the vignettes that are created.

In addition to the considerations regarding first, second and third language usage in vignettes, multi- and monolingual environments, and the various dialects within languages, may also inform the vignettes that are crafted. Dialects may convey meanings that are particular to specific regions and may also vary in terms of word usage. For instance, the words 'French fries' or 'pacifier' in American English would be 'chips' and 'dummy' in British English. When a vignette is crafted, these variations will need to be taken into consideration.

The unique nature of vignette observations/perceptions

Although the uniqueness of the nature of vignette observations with regard to perceptions is quite clear, a distinction can also be made between 'observation' and 'perception'. In the IVR school of thought, the idea is that 'observation' encapsulates some degree of preconceived ideas, whereas the intention with 'perception' is to enter the research site with an openness that is encouraged in all the phases of vignette research. Vignette observation is about opening up perceptual awareness of the co-experiential experience as much as possible. It also relates to the awareness within vignette researchers, as they create experiential protocols, of the need to refrain from imposing their own ideas on the experience, and instead to perceive the experience for what it is.

In many research methods, observations are usually an auxiliary data collection strategy, whereas in vignette research, they are the primary method of data collection. It is thus worth considering the elevation and amplification of observation as a data collection strategy in vignette research. Observations within vignette research are similar, yet also distinct from general observational data collection strategies in related research methods. Observations may occasionally be structured, but are mostly unstructured in order to optimize the capture of experiences. Vignette observations can also be simultaneously structured and unstructured.

Vignette observations are 'unstructured' when a vignette researcher enters the research field with an open attitude. They may become more structured as the researcher starts to notice certain themes emerging in the context and the vignette notes take on more internal organization. They may also remain completely unstructured throughout the period of co-experiential experience, leaving the vignette researcher with a set of detailed observation notes from which 'structure' will only emerge when the raw vignette is created.

Vignette observations are 'structured' when a vignette researcher decides the themes or phenomena on which data will be collected. The researcher may, for instance, create a template relating to certain dimensions of a phenomenon that they wish to explore. Predominantly though, most vignette researchers tend to enter the research field with an open mind (and heart) in order to capture the phenomenon as it presents itself, rather than shaping phenomena through preconceived ideas in an observation schedule.

The uniqueness of vignette observations is also evident in the participant-observer continuum. In most qualitative research methods, researchers declare their status as either 'participant-observer' or 'observer-participant', thereby indicating the emphasis placed on the specific sides of the role. Many vignette researchers decline this binary definition within their co-experiential activities, because they are again adopting the full continuum of roles simultaneously. In their view, the vignette researcher is an active observer while simultaneously also being an active participant in the experience, but not necessarily overtly involved in the activities. For instance, if a vignette researcher is observing an art lesson, they will not be creating a painting themselves, but rather observing those who are painting. The vignette researcher seeks to capture the co-experiential experience in all its intimacy and intricacy, and therefore should not be considered as a minor or 'lesser' participant. Vignette research seeks to decrease the distance inherent in the participant-observer continuum.

Many vignette researchers are, however, also of the view that vignette observations are markedly that of a participant-observer – with no room for being a 'participant'. They argue that the moment that a vignette researcher becomes a participant, they would not be capturing the experiences of the others anymore, but rather some version of their own participation in the dynamics or the event.

Time, space, relationships and corporeality

As with writers of literary genres, vignette researchers pay attention to the ways in which time, space, relationships and corporeality are present within a vignette. In order for these dimensions of the co-experiential experience to be present in a final vignette, they need to be captured at the point of observation. Therefore, in addition to 'following their attention', a vignette researcher will also take note of the dimensions of traditional storytelling. When and where is this experience taking place? When, where and how is this phenomenon manifesting? The vignette researcher needs to guide the reader into the world of the experience by leaving clues in the text about time and place. In this regard, the vignette researcher could give descriptions of real time, as well as perceived time. In some vignettes, therefore, it may be that time is dragging, whereas in others, time may be flying – and is then depicted as such. Similarly, the vignette researcher needs to reflect the relationships between the role players in the vignette. Who is present in the vignette? How do they relate to one another? What are the interpersonal dynamics in the vignette? Who is a prominent figure in the vignette?

In this regard, the corporeality of the co-experiential experience being depicted is of utmost importance. In what way is this 'experience experienced' within the body of the person portrayed in the vignette? The German descriptor would be *Zwischenleiblichkeit* or in English 'intercorporeality'. The notion of intercorporeality has been explored intensively at a theoretical level and 'stresses the role of embodied interactions between the self and the other in the process of social understanding' (Tanaka 2015: 455). Within descriptions of intercorporeality, the researcher therefore seeks to capture primordial empathy, to create interactional synchrony and engender a deep sense of mutual understanding, agitating against the limitations that are often encountered by mental representations of meaning and experience (Tanaka 2015). At the practical level, this means that vignette researchers create the meaning of an experience directly and in the moment.

Writing your raw vignette

'Show, don't tell'

Writing vignettes as a researcher is both an art and a scientific process. It is the art of depicting an experience that might not otherwise be captured or presented in this particular way, but it is also a process of scientific writing. The vignette researcher uses the notes from the experiential protocols, which were captured in the field, as the basis for crafting the first raw vignette. The raw vignette represents the next level of data analysis within the vignette research process. In vignette research, data analysis begins at the point of data collection. When the vignette researcher starts to collect data, the data analysis process has effectively commenced due to the selective attention of the vignette researcher. In crafting the vignette, the vignette researcher 'shows' the phenomenon, rather than 'telling' the reader what to think about the phenomenon. Withholding judgement is therefore key to the creation of the vignette. The vignette researcher seeks instead to present the experience in a way that is as close as possible, descriptively, to what the actual experience entailed, then intentionally leaves the interpretive dimension to the reader.

'How does this phenomenon reveal itself?' or 'How is it showing itself to me?' During the creation of the experiential protocol, these questions may assist the vignette researcher to co-experientially experience in a way that will limit interpretation and optimize intercorporeality. For instance, rather than stating that 'she looks tired' (which would be an interpretation), the vignette researcher would state that 'her eyes are drooping', or 'she closes her eyes slowly', thereby capturing the physical actions. The vignette researcher is thus constantly asking: What is the observational evidence that reveals the experience?

Equally important to the capture of intercorporeality is the read-across between the observations/perceptions and the vignette. There needs to be a high level of read-across between a vignette researcher's observation notes and the vignette that is written on the basis of them. Thus, all the elements in the vignette need to be rooted in the raw data, namely the observation notes. For instance, if a vignette states, 'She wears a light blue T-shirt and has a high ponytail', there need to be observation notes that describe the participant as wearing a light blue T-shirt and having a high ponytail. If the vignette states that a teacher is whispering something to a class, the observation notes need to indicate it.

In 'showing' the phenomenon in this way, the vignette researcher seeks to transport the reader to the exact moment of the experience. In the same way that a literary writer would 'show' a character, a place, an interaction or a moment in time, the vignette research writer 'shows' the phenomenon under study. What differentiates the vignette of a researcher from a fictional vignette, however, is its rootedness in the raw data, and the subsequent processes that validate and authenticate the presentation of research findings. A literary writer may base a vignette on fictional experiences, but the vignettes of a vignette researcher can always be traced back to the raw data, which originated in co-experiential experience. As with all scientific writing, the process of vignette research is grounded in raw data and theoretical assumptions. Vignette 10 illustrates the fidelity between the raw vignette and the observation notes in the researcher's experimental protocol. Some of the correlations are underlined in the vignette, and then marked in red in Figure 5 and Figure 6 which depict a section of the observation notes:

Vignette 10: 'The crutches'

> She gently puts down her crutches on the floor, close to the table and away from the aisle. The chemistry teacher tells everyone what to fetch from the cabinets at the back of the classroom for the experiments. She goes to the other corner of the classroom and sits down with four of her friends. As she sits there, the crutches are kicked and stepped on by several classmates who do not see them on the ground. One other student picks up the crutches and hops around the class with the crutches. They put them back on the floor. The chemistry experiments on acidity continue. Some students consult the huge periodic table at the front of the classroom. The wide orange curtains in the room are drawn against the snowy weather outside the classroom. She is 14 years old. She sits with a black-and-white, short-sleeved Adidas T-shirt and completes all the tables in front of her with her friends. When she is done, she takes the clip from her head and reties her ponytail. She moves back to her original seat; her right foot is in a big plastic medical boot. When she sits down, she picks up her crutches and instead of putting them down on the floor, she balances them at an angle so that half of the aisle is blocked. The aisle is blocked, but she can reach the crutches easily. It is clean-up time after the chemistry lesson. The students are walking up and down the aisle to put away the materials. Now, no one steps on, or bumps into, the crutches that are blocking half of the aisle at the back of the class.

> Vignette writer: Irma Eloff, 2019, Masterclass in Vignette writing, University of Innsbruck, Austria, unpublished.

The high level of read-across between the experience, the observations/perceptions and the final vignettes in the IVR project is a clear departure from the use of fictional vignettes in earlier

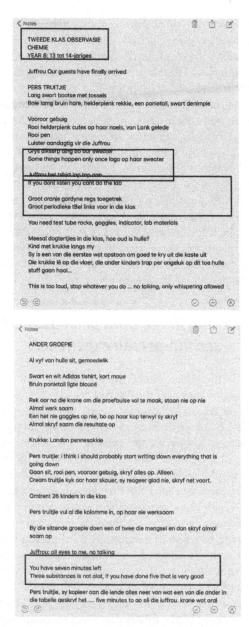

FIGURES 5 and 6 *Section of observation notes written in English and in the vignette researcher's first language (Afrikaans).*
Source: Authors

vignette research (Hughes and Huby 2004). Some researchers (Constant, Kiesler and Sproull 1994; Kirmayer, Fletcher and Boothroyd 1997) have utilized vignettes to facilitate other data collection strategies. These same researchers have, however, raised concerns about the use of hypothetical content in vignettes and have also commented on the various levels of fictionality within vignettes that may potentially influence research findings. In the IVR school of thought, vignettes are never fictional or hypothetical but are deeply rooted in real-life experiences. In the case of hypothetical or fictional vignettes, the indications are that 'a vignette character may prompt a response based on ideas about how some person known to participants would be likely to respond, rather than giving their own reactions' (Hughes and Huby 2004). The IVR vignettes can be traced to specific, real experiences. Where IVR uses vignettes as prompts, these vignettes are also based on real-life experiences. Each experience is regarded as unique and not as a prototype for particular situations or issues.

Writing in the third person about second-person experiences

First-person writing has gained significant traction in qualitative research methodologies over the last few decades (Denzin and Lincoln 2011). Vignette research, however, aligns more strongly with what Churchill (2012: 1) terms 'second-person perspectivity'. Writing in the third person about second-person experiences is a distinct characteristic of the IVR school of thought. It is a methodology for 'those who would seek to understand not only their own "first person" experiences but also the first person experiences of others' (Churchill 2012: 1). Vignette researchers seek to capture the experience of the other by attempting to describe embodied experiences (see also 'Intersubjectivity of research' section). A third-person writing style is therefore proactively adopted in vignette research. The vignette researcher writes the vignette from the perspective of the other and resists the temptation to superimpose their own views onto that of the other through a first-person account. Vignettes are therefore written using the pronouns 'he/she/it/they'. In order to make their vignettes relatable, however, vignette researchers are encouraged to assign names (anonymized) to the characters in their vignettes, even as they write in the third person. The IVR researchers do value the impact and magnitude of first-person accounts in qualitative research and applaud the compelling case that has been made for autoethnographic vignettes (Humphreys 2005). However, in the IVR school of thought, the vignette researcher seeks to offer an alternative route to understanding phenomena and the experiences of others, through the use of third-person writing in vignettes.

In general, there are three types of third-person writing styles that are relevant to vignette writing: third-person objective, third-person limited and third-person omniscient. In the third-person objective writing style, the vignette writer tells the story in a slightly distant way by means of solely 'neutral' observations. In the third-person limited writing style, the vignette writer narrates purely from the viewpoint of one person, adding only limited details. In the third-person omniscient writing style, the vignette writer gives the impression of being widely knowledgeable about the situation, will demonstrate familiarity with wide-ranging contextual details, may shift the storytelling between different players in the vignette and also share insights from multiple perspectives.

The three types of third-person writing are illustrated by the following examples. Third-person objective might read: 'The couple was on the balcony after dancing together to lively music. The moon was shining through the leaves of the large oak tree and the night sounds wrapped around them like a blanket.' An example of the third-person limited style might be: 'Jessica saw that Magdalena was enjoying herself. She was smiling and chatting to her dance partner. Jessica smiled as she looked at the two of them.' Third-person omniscient narration might run as follows: 'Magdalena was elated. She had danced all evening and everyone was captivated by her glowing countenance. Peter was engrossed in their conversation on the balcony as they were catching their breaths after a particularly lively salsa.'

The choice between these writing styles and the degree to which each of them is adopted in the vignette is up to the vignette writer. The original contextual experience will also be relevant to the decision.

Creating mood and atmosphere in the vignette

Vignette researchers need to create the atmosphere of the experience for their readers, and this needs to be achieved within a concise text. The brevity of the vignette is both an opportunity and a challenge.

The reader needs to be transported to the experience and feel the experience. How does this vignette make you feel? This may be a good question to ask after writing the first draft of the vignette in the context of resonance reading (see 'Presenting your raw vignette' and 'Resonance reading' sections). Is the pathos of the experience adequately articulated? If not, how can it be improved?

Vignette researchers create an atmosphere by using a range of writing strategies. Sensory details, rich descriptions, attention to precise word usage and sentence structures, and metaphors, similes and analogies are just some of the options. The use of extensive and detailed observation notes as a basis for text creation is an integral feature of vignette research; these also help the vignette researcher create a specific atmosphere. The rich sensory details that are captured in the observation notes can be infused throughout the vignette text. Describing the flight of a bird against the bright blue sky, the slow smell of coffee in a tiny kitchen, the crunch of well-worn leather boots on a gravel road or the way in which rain droplets are trickling down a window pane creates a picture in the mind of the reader. Such descriptions may make the need for explicit explanations of the experience redundant, thereby serving one of the primary purposes of vignette research – to 'show, rather than tell'.

Paying careful attention to every word choice and to sentence structure is another strategy that influences the atmosphere created in a vignette. Playing around with sentence structures, and using synonyms and antonyms in different versions of the vignette, may also generate atmosphere. In this regard, the length of sentences can also be a key vehicle through which the affective dimension of a vignette is developed. Do you want to create a sense of urgency? Play around with short, staccato sentences. Do you want to convey a sense of long-windedness? Try to stretch the sentences in the vignette to see how that affects the atmosphere.

The use of metaphors, similes or analogies can also conjure certain visual images that contribute to the atmosphere the vignette researcher is trying to create. 'Soft as a petal', 'sharp as a needle', or 'high as a mountain' can convey a message that would otherwise take up several sentences. 'It was music to his ears', or 'drowning in a sea of paperwork', or 'a rollercoaster of emotions' are similar examples of descriptions that may be inserted into the vignette.

Vignette researchers also give considered thought to sensory descriptors in the vignette text. Describing an experience in terms of the five senses is integral to a vignette. Visual words (sense of sight), auditory or acoustic words (sense of sound), tactile words (sense of touch), gustatory words (sense of taste) and olfactory words (sense of smell) enrich the vignette and recreate the experience in the mind of the reader. In addition to the basic sensory descriptors in a vignette, the senses may also be described in more detail and depth. For instance, the tactile sensation of an old table may be described using words such as 'rough', 'smooth', 'sticky', or 'worn'. However, tactile sensations can also be refined further by adding thermal sensations (warm, hot, cold, icy), moisture sensations (wet, dry, damp), or weight and pressure sensations (heavy, light, wobbly).

In addition to the five senses, kinaesthetic words may also be used to enrich descriptions and create an atmosphere in a vignette. Table 2 provides some examples of sensory and kinaesthetic descriptors. Expansive lists of similar descriptors are available in all major languages.

TABLE 2 Examples of sensory and kinaesthetic descriptors

Category	Examples of descriptors
Visual words (sense of sight)	Bright, vibrant, opaque, dim, gleaming, polished, reflective, twinkling, never-ending
Auditory or acoustic words (sense of sound)	Bubbling, whirring, purring, silent, serene, deafening, boisterous, calming
Tactile words (sense of touch)	Soft, supple, pliable, smooth, silky, velvety, rough, coarse, spiky, icy, plush
Gustatory words (sense of taste)	Sweet, sugary, honeyed, salty, briny, sour, tart, nutty, fruity, vinegary, tangy, tasty, delicious
Olfactory words (sense of smell)	Smoky, fresh, scorched, charred, washed, fragrant, perfumed, balmy, musky, scented, spicy
Kinaesthetic words (kinaesthesia)	Rushing, soothing, approaching, escaping, sitting, standing, leaning, crouching, tilting, looming, meeting

Source: Authors

In the same way as they give careful consideration to sensory descriptors, vignette researchers may also actively seek a rich repertoire of synonyms for their vignettes. For instance, instead of merely stating, 'She says', a vignette researcher may also choose to say, 'She blurts out', 'She gently whispers', 'She declares', 'She announces', 'She divulges', 'She affirms' or any one of a plethora of synonyms that will add richness to the vignette.

Unique insights and nuance

A vignette researcher seeks to present a unique insight about a phenomenon in a vignette. A vignette should intentionally not be presented 'traditionally', but rather be geared towards challenging views of a situation and the reporter's perspective. As a methodological choice, vignette studies present the researcher with an opportunity to offer insights and perspectives that might not easily be accessible via other research methodologies. Even though vignettes are brief, they need to provide the reader with a moment of pause and reflection. Some vignettes are surprising. Other vignettes confirm insights that have been presented elsewhere, but articulate them in a new way.

Vignettes can utilize a wide variety of literary tools and techniques to convey an experience or phenomenon. There can be plot twists, contrasts, irony, dialogue, extended metaphors or foreshadowing. The vignette researcher may use humour, imagery, analogy, paradoxes, personification or even satire to craft the vignette. Literary techniques such as symbolism, hyperbole, suspense, allegory, allusions or anachronism can be employed to emphasize particular aspects in the vignette and to amplify an experience. Some vignettes may contain a potent *Aha-Erlebnis*, an experience that brings a distinct insight or surprise. Vignette researchers can also use alliteration, assonance or onomatopoeia, using words to create a vivid and immediate picture in the mind of the vignette reader. In short narratives such as vignettes, juxtaposition can also convey precise meaning within a short sentence or two, and motifs and flashbacks can similarly be used to pack immense meaning into a few sentences. Some vignette researchers may also use anastrophe, where traditional sentence structures are reversed ('In the summer sky shimmered the moon'), and also anaphora, where a similar word or phrase is repeated and adapted at the beginning of a sentence ('It was the best of times, it was the worst of times'). Such literary tools can have great effect. Correspondingly, the universally accepted truths contained in aphorisms ('Actions speak louder than words') may also be used to show the key message of a vignette and open it up to a wider audience. Some vignette researchers also use colloquialism, inserting casual language into their writing, to convey a mood or an atmosphere. For instance, 'She is wearing cool sunglasses and a chic T-shirt', he exclaims, creates an informal atmosphere that may communicate the message the vignette researcher is trying to convey. In short, there are numerous literary tools that a vignette researcher may utilize to convey atmosphere and to distil descriptions. Vignette researchers pay specific attention to the nuances that are conveyed in the vignette. What are the feelings and emotions that a vignette elicits from the reader? What is the atmosphere that is created? Which lines of thought are sparked in the mind of the vignette reader?

In writing the first raw vignette, the vignette researcher is constantly asking questions. In what ways are the phenomena revealing themselves within this context? How can I portray that? Writing a vignette is about portraying the embodied experience of the other. In doing so, the vignette researcher attempts to capture the uniqueness of the other's experience and the infinitesimal nuances within that experience.

Free writing and the length of vignettes

The initial process of writing the raw vignette should ideally focus on free writing. This phase is about getting as much as possible into the text of the vignette, and during it, generativity surpasses perfection. The priority is to generate a raw vignette text, even though it might not be a perfect first draft.

The process of vignette writing is, in essence, iterative. There are several rounds of editing, revising and recrafting. The feedback and suggestions provided by others are integral to the creation of a vignette (see 'Presenting your raw vignette' section). During the initial writing phase, the vignette researcher writes a first draft. The length of the vignette varies from one vignette writer to another. Some vignette researchers suggest a length between around half a page and a maximum of one page. Some vignette researchers actively caution against vignettes becoming too lengthy and thereby detracting from the primary focus of the vignette. In such instances, an initial raw vignette may often be divided into two or even three vignettes. During the subsequent phases, this first draft will be revised continuously, and the length of the vignette may be adjusted accordingly.

Example of a long vignette:

Vignette 11: 'Hope'

> The room itself is dull, shaded with yellow walls and yellow lights. However, Rose's energy fills the space with an overwhelming yet all-embracing and encompassing sense of warmth, love and acceptance. Her smile is comforting. She speaks about her experiences of hope metaphorically, likening the phenomenon to a hurricane. She explains that hope is the eye of a hurricane and coming to a place of peace requires one to undergo the turbulence of life's many storms. Whilst twirling her foot around in a circular motion, she notes that how you choose to face the trials and tribulations of the storms ahead and what you do with your pain and hurt decides your life trajectory. Without saying a word, her deep eye contact seems to explain all that she is feeling. She explains that she is hard on herself and, in the same breath, she laughs it off as if it doesn't matter. She remembers a time in her life when she experienced emotional detachment from her traumas with a sense of discomfort. She scratches her knee. Shrugging her shoulders and exhaling, she smiles; sharing that through COVID-dictated self-isolation and subsequent spiritual reflection, she has come to know and love herself in faith. There is a moment when a ray of light shines through the window, casting a light on Rose. Poised in stature and soft in tone, she speaks about searching for the light at the end of the tunnel. She speaks about finding herself through her struggles. Whilst stating positive self-affirmations, she expresses the realization that she is her own source of hope and strength.
>
> Vignette writer: Megan Lynn Swart, 2021, University of Pretoria, South Africa, unpublished revised vignette from MEd dissertation (Swart 2021: 51).

Example of a short vignette:

Vignette 12: 'Teachers'

> Enrica smiles as she speaks. The breakout group discussion is winding down. 'Teachers are very, very tired for another project and another project,' she says. She looks straight into the camera. Her face fills most of the screen. A bright green line runs all around the block that frames her face as she speaks. The inside of her jacket is fluffy. 'Mmmmmm . . .' Enrica murmurs. 'They are very, very tired from all the extra work,' she reiterates.
>
> Vignette writer: Irma Eloff, 2021, Teach4Reach
webinar, hosted by the University of Vienna,
Austria, unpublished.

As with literary writing, the vignette researcher may potentially encounter stumbling blocks during this initial phase. Often, this 'writer's block' may be constructively interpreted as a pointer 'to leave one place behind and arrive someplace else' (McKerracher 2019: 7), to find new ways of seeing and interpreting. The iterative nature of vignette writing in research can assist by ensuring researchers remain open to the views of others throughout the process. The vignette researcher may also utilize the strategies deployed by literary writers to overcome writer's block, such as going for a walk, sleeping on it, deliberately writing anything that comes to mind, or even staying at the table until something is written. These strategies will be highly personal for each vignette writer.

Providing a title for your vignette

You will have noticed the short titles given to the preceding example vignettes. Vignettes are sometimes untitled, but where a title is created it should preferably be neutral. The rationale for this is to leave the emphasis on the content of the vignette and the experience that the vignette is attempting to convey, that is, meaning should be communicated within the vignette itself and not in the 'catchiness' of a title that might distract the reader's attention. In some instances, the vignette researcher may even opt to provide basic numerical titles: 'Vignette 1', 'Vignette 2', and so forth. The vignettes may also be titled by data set within a research project: 'Vignette A, interviews, Tyrol', or 'Vignette C, sustainability workshop, Pretoria'. A vignette title may also comprise the anonymized or real names (where consents were provided) of the participants, for example, Sarah, Christina, Marilyn or their titles and surnames, e.g. Herr Wagner, Mr Smith or Dr Du Plessis.

Some vignette researchers ask their resonance reading group (see 'Presenting your raw vignette' and 'Resonance reading' sections) to provide a title for the vignette under discussion. This strategy may provide insight into the ways in which a vignette is perceived, and it may also assist the vignette researcher to align the intent of the vignette (what it reveals) with the content of the vignette.

Editing your raw vignette

After having crafted the first raw vignette, the vignette researcher may opt to engage in a process of self-editing. Read through the vignette. Read it aloud or read it silently. Read it several times. Assess and evaluate the sentence construction. Refine the sentences. Are there any repetitions that need to be reformulated or deleted? Is there any word usage that can be improved? Are the sentences clear? In editing the vignette, the vignette researcher should be reminded that a vignette needs to convey a message all of its own, even if no prior or subsequent context is provided. It is a clear and distinct narrative that can be read independently from other texts. The message of the vignette is also implicit, rather than explicit (e.g. 'show, don't tell'). The vignette researcher seeks to make the experience speak for itself within the vignette.

Vignettes present a recreation rather than a reconstruction of an experience. In a reconstruction, the vignette writer would add layers of interpretation into the vignette. In a recreation of an experience, the vignette researcher attempts to recreate the actual experience as closely as possible. The reader needs to feel the experience as it happened. Vignettes also embrace ambiguity. It is not within the ambit of the vignette to necessarily provide clarity, although it may do so inadvertently. Providing clarity is not the primary purpose of a vignette, however. This is rather to convey the co-experiential experience in all its richness, which may in many ways include ambiguity, uncertainty and vulnerability.

Presenting your raw vignette

After writing and editing the raw vignette, vignette researchers present it to an audience of their choosing. This audience may include the participants in the study, fellow vignette researchers and professionals in the field of study, or a combination of individuals who will be able to provide comments on the raw vignette. It may also include a PLC or a community of practice. This phase builds on the notion of debate within scientific communities, but the discussion does not have to be with/within a scientific community.

The presentation of a raw vignette is known as a 'resonance reading' (see also the 'Resonance reading' section). At the first resonance reading, the vignette researcher asks for open and frank feedback from a group. This is an opportunity to clarify, strengthen and refine the vignette, improving on the original version. Members of the group may even be invited to rewrite or rephrase certain sentences and sections of the vignette. This strategy enables the vignette researcher to comprehend more fully how others understood the vignette. The resonance that is created by a vignette is a critical ingredient of the vignette itself, but also of the process of communicating the co-experiential experience. At the resonance reading the vignette researcher reads the raw vignette out loud. A written copy of the raw vignette may have been made available to the audience prior to the resonance reading. The resonance group (e.g. audience) is asked specifically about the elements and aspects of the vignette that resonated with them personally. During this feedback, the vignette researcher makes detailed notes on the comments that are made. Taking the feedback as their basis, the vignette researcher revisits the vignette and refines it further.

Questions 1–10 are examples of questions that may be put to the resonance group to elicit feedback:

1 What are your first impressions of the vignette?

2 What resonated with you?

3 What did the vignette make you think of?

4 Would you suggest any changes to the vignette?

5 Would you make any additions or deletions to the text of the vignette?

6 Are there any aspects of the vignette that are not clear to you?

7 Are you comfortable with the words and phrases that are
   used in the vignette? Do you have any suggestions for
   alternative formulations?
8 Which parts of the vignette specifically resonate with you?
9 What parts of the vignette still need to be strengthened or
   clarified?
10 Do you have any final comments on the vignette?

Some vignette researchers record the feedback that is provided
during a resonance reading, in order to be able to revisit the
comments. In conjunction with detailed written or typed notes,
recordings can serve as a valuable resource for the vignette
researcher when crafting the final vignette.

It is the prerogative of the vignette researchers to decide on the
extent to which he/she will incorporate the comments from the
resonance group into the final text of the vignette. The vignette
researcher is the writer of the vignette and will therefore have the
final say over the vignette. For instance, in a vignette that depicts
students lounging outside between lectures, a member of a resonance
group might have asked for more details on why some students
are alone. The vignette researcher may decide to leave this aspect
implicit. In a vignette on a youth games night, a member of a
resonance group might have commented that it seemed chaotic; in
this case the vignette writer may decide to provide more clarity in the
description.

Revising and refining your vignette

After the resonance reading, the vignette researcher conducts a pre-
final revision of the vignette. The vignette researcher reflects on the
feedback and comments, revises the text and then prepares the text
for presentation to the research participants. The pre-final vignette is
presented to the participants in a format that may be similar to that
of the vignette resonance reading. Ideally, this reading will take place
in person, in order to enable the verbal and non-verbal responses of
the participants to the vignette to be communicated. Where in-
person resonance readings are not possible, the resonance reading
may also be conducted online. In both instances, the resonance

reading should be recorded. The responses from participants constitute a valuable data source for the vignette researcher. Since it is the intention of the vignette researcher to present a co-experiential experience, it is critical that there is a high level of read-across between the experience of the participants and the way in which the experience is presented in the vignette (see section entitled 'Writing your raw vignette'). Hovewer, it is the *co*-experiential experience of the vignette writer, so also in this phase of the process he/she will decide on the extent to which the comments from the participants into the final text of the vignette will be incorparated. Many vignette writers have also experienced that they perceive the experiences of others more strongly or somehow different than the participants themselves, who sometimes cannot remember the experience at all. Vignette researchers can ask themselves the following questions to help them refine the final vignette:

1   Does the vignette convey a specific message? Does it provide a glimpse into my participant's life? Does it show something in particular?

2   Who 'tells the story' in my vignette? Does it remain consistent throughout the vignette? If the perspective of the storyteller shifts in the vignette, is this intentional and does it make sense?

3   What is the atmosphere that is created by my vignette? Vignettes are about creating atmosphere/pathos/shared experience, in addition to the details of the 'story'. Does my vignette convey a specific atmosphere?

4   Does my vignette reduce the distance between the 'observer'/'perceiver' and the main 'character' in the vignette? Vignettes are about shortening the distance between researcher and participant. Is my vignette achieving this? When you read my vignette, do you feel as if you are 'in the shoes' of the person being written about?

5   After I have given some thought to my vignette (sometimes a good night's sleep can help with this), is there any way in which I can further strengthen my vignette?

6   Do I need to shuffle the order of the sentences inside the vignette, in order to strengthen the 'golden thread' of the story or scene?

7   Does my vignette use sensory descriptions to enrich the story? (These could be visual, auditory, tactile, olfactory and perhaps even gustatory, for example corporeality/bodily experience.)

8   Does my vignette provide a clear description of place, so that my reader can 'picture' where the vignette is situated?

9   Have I checked the vignette for technical fluency and accuracy, punctuation marks, grammar and so forth?

10 Is there any redundant text in my vignette, repetition or similar words being used more than once?

11 Have I checked my text for sentences that may be too long? Mixing up short and longer sentences can work well in a vignette.

12 Can I condense my vignette in any way? Vignettes are about the creation of a short, impactful text. Can I remove any details that are not central to my vignette?

13 Have I checked my observation notes and experiential protocols, to see if there is anything that I can add to or revise in my vignette?

14 When I finish reading my vignette, am I left with a particular feeling? Am I affected by reading the vignette?

In revising and refining the final vignette, the vignette researcher may invite the participants to suggest changes to the vignette or offer improvements to assist readers to understand the gist of the vignette, using these questions. The participants may make adjustments to the text if they feel the need to do so. This recursive process may be repeated as many times as necessary. We would strongly suggest that in the end, there should be a collective sense that the vignette is 'complete'. Vignette 13 illustrates how final technical edits can be made to a vignette. In this example, only one sentence has been slightly adjusted:

Vignette 13: 'Andreas, Julia and the trash can'

It's a warm Thursday afternoon and the sun is shining; the sky is blue. There is no wind, and the birds are singing. Tall alders grow along a farm track. The sun shines through the leaves of the alders, creating a pleasant alternation between sun and shade. The field path is used by many hikers on this beautiful spring day. In the middle of the farm track is a bench with a trash can where people can rest after a long walk or hike. Andreas passes by with his dog, which is barking. He holds a paper bag in his left hand and the dog's leash in his right. The paper bag is neatly filled with waste, such as newspapers, wrappers and beverage cans. When Andreas sees the trash can, he walks straight towards it and tries to stuff the paper bag into the can. The trash can is much too small. The paper bag tears and the garbage falls to the ground. Hectically, he tries to stuff the things back into the garbage can, but it is just overflowing. After unsuccessfully collecting the trash, Andreas gives up and leaves the beverage cans and packaging on the floor under and around the trash can. After looking around to see if anyone saw him, he walks on with his dog. Nothing happens for five minutes. Suddenly Julia appears. She immediately sees the mess next to the bench and goes straight to it. Shaking her head, she now stands in front of the trash can. Julia opens her jacket and pulls out a garbage bag. She opens it and quickly collects all the trash from the ground. Julia also empties the trash can. She ties the trash bag and swings it over her right shoulder. Whistling, she walks back in the direction from which she came.

Vignette writer: Bernhard Nairz, 2022, Master student assignment on Sustainability, Aldrans, Austria, unpublished.

The final vignette and communicative validation

When do you know that your vignette is complete? A vignette is finished when the iterative process of communicative validation has been concluded. The vignette needs to 'ring true' within the resonance group reading, and there need to be high levels of acceptance within this group, indicating that the vignette is indeed depicting the experience, as it was experienced. However, even though vignettes are a collective effort in terms of the invitational nature of the underlying creative process, it is ultimately the vignette writer who decides if a version of the vignette is final. It is the vignette researcher who considers all the inputs, and then determines what constitutes the final vignette.

How do you know that you have a 'final' vignette? There is a sense of completeness. This sense of completeness may come shortly after or even during the resonance reading, or it may come after some time has elapsed and you have considered the feedback from the resonance group members. Glenn Doman (1990: 265) has remarked: 'It has been said that the only two difficult things about writing a book are to write the first sentence and to write the last sentence.' In many ways, the same is true of vignettes. Deciding when a vignette is final can be a critical decision, and in the world of research it may immeasurably affect the ways in which the world is understood.

CHAPTER FOUR

Analysing Vignettes

Vignettes are not analysed or interpreted in a conventional way. Rather, the aim is to value the fullness and richness of experience articulated in a vignette and to show this abundance in as many facets as possible and in different readings. Depending on the reading and the reader, other things come to light and into view. One thing may be in view, while other things may remain in the shadows. This chapter explains how readers relate to vignettes and how they might respond to the demands they make on them. Two processes are described: (i) resonance readings, where vignettes are read aloud to a group to obtain their insights and feedback; and (ii) vignette readings, which focus mostly on the text of the vignette and which can be undertaken individually and in written format, or in a group. Just as the researcher co-experientially experiences the experiences in the field, the vignette's dense description triggers a resonance in readers that highlights their experiences. This can manifest itself in a sense of wonder and amazement as we read, when the experiences articulated touch and affect us. The chapter concludes with a specific example to illustrate the process of reading vignettes.

Vignettes are analysed in two steps or processes: resonance reading and vignette reading. Resonance readings and vignette readings may take place interchangeably, in any order and as many times as is deemed necessary. It should be noted though that a raw vignette is only finished and transformed into a final vignette after the resonance reading. The resonance reading (see 'Resonance reading' section) usually comes first, and can also include some form of data processing as discussed in the 'Presenting your raw vignette' section. The second step, the vignette reading, involves writing down the experiences of reading the vignette in the form of a *text*. Here the feedback is written, whereas feedback in a resonance reading tends to be verbal and delivered in person and in real time. However, other forms of non-text-based analysis can also be undertaken (in a group), for example, through a discursive (Agostini 2016b) or scenic vignette reading (Peterlini 2017) (see 'Vignette reading' section). Let's start with a systematic description of resonance reading, which provides complementary information to the 'Presenting your raw vignette' section. This further focus on resonance reading should make it clear that we are already in the middle of the process of analysing vignettes.

Resonance reading

Researchers record signs or indicators of experiences in the field by which the vignette writers are affected, or 'struck' and which they condense into raw narrative vignettes as soon as possible after the data has been collected. In the subsequent process of resonance reading, the raw vignettes are discussed in a (research) group/PLC and/or with the participants in the field and are – through intersubjective or communicative validation – enriched and condensed. During the process of resonance reading, the participants are asked to describe the situation from their own point of view. However, the vignette writers always retain control of the narrative – after all, it is their intersubjective experience. At this stage of the process, the account can be supplemented with contextual information or quotes, or corrected if necessary. The aim of intersubjective validation is not to reconstruct the experience as a whole, searching for the 'truth' of a case, but rather to clarify the language and the experiential context. Just as in the final vignette, the raw vignette should ideally shed light on three questions:

1 What is happening? The focus is on the sequence of events, facts and actions.

2 How is it happening? The focus is on the pathic aspects, i.e. the disruptive or unsettling moments of the described and tangible experience.

3 What is affecting me as a reader? The focus is on the response to what is happening; this can of course vary, or may need to vary, in the course of the resonance reading.

Revision focuses in particular on how the experience perceived in the context of the situation can be translated into language as pithily as possible (Agostini et al. 2023a: 41).

1 Does the vignette communicate the atmosphere?
2 Does it retain the co-affective experience?
3 Is the situation relatable?
4 Can some passages be omitted?
5 What is non-essential?

The words used must thus be given careful consideration. The important thing is that it is less about demonstration, and more about gesturing towards what has been perceived and co-experientially experienced. The words, sentences or passages chosen to express what is co-experientially experienced, perceived or heard in the atmosphere bring the vignette to life, and in this context particular attention is paid to the language of the body. This process can also deal with questions—for instance, how the vignettes presented in this book could have tied the experiences even more closely to the bodily expressions of the participants and used adjectives as thoughtfully as possible to adequately describe the events. The point of the co-experiential experience at which the vignette begins and ends is often also important, as this influences the meaning of the narrative. Thus, the art of writing vignettes is to make experiences linguistically present so that they can be *re*-experienced by readers (Agostini 2017: 26–9), while at the same time maintaining the ambiguity of the vignette, i.e., avoiding interpretation. Only after this intersubjective review is the vignette finalized and researchers can start the process of analysis, which in vignette research is referred to as vignette reading.

Vignette reading

Vignette reading entails the reading of a vignette and providing written responses, and can be undertaken by an individual on their own. We use the example of Vignette 3 here to illustrate the process of vignette reading. At the end of the chapter there is also a sample vignette reading for Vignette 8 (from Agostini 2016b: 55–62).

Vignette 3: 'On the pavement'

> A young woman is striding along the pavement, throwing her arms alternately back and forth, her head moving slightly back and forth, and briefly craning her neck. On the cycle lane immediately to the left, a cyclist comes towards her, his gaze fixed on the woman coming towards him. Almost imperceptibly, her step becomes stiffer, she turns her head slightly to the right; the swinging of her head to either side that accompanies the walking step freezes. The cyclist's gaze remains fixed on the woman for a moment, then, as they pass each other, he turns his head to the other side.
>
> PETERLINI 2020: 29

The vignette describes a scene as it might be perceived on the street any day and is therefore very recognizable. Is an experience happening here? How and in what form does it manifest itself? A young woman strides along the pavement, attracting the attention of a cyclist. In response, her attitude changes, 'her step becomes stiffer, she turns her head slightly to the right; the swinging of her head to either side that accompanies the walking step freezes'. Reading the short scene, it becomes clear that looks contain offers of relationships. While the man keeps his gaze fixed on the woman, she averts her gaze. She seems not to respond to his offer.

Responses to different experiences in vignettes can be understood from joint readings of vignettes, either discursive (Agostini 2016b) or scenic (Peterlini 2017). Only written readings, however, put researchers in a position to once again take an experiential approach towards this new reading experience. Thus, in writing down the vignette readings, they are engaging with a situation that is about making, reflecting and actualizing past experiences (Rieger-Ladich 2014: 353–4). In linking to this bodily and sensuous experience, written expression thus mediates between experiential reality and conceptual thinking. In order to gain access to co-experiential experience and to be able to understand the meaning of experience, researchers are dependent on such linguistic expression (Meyer-

Drawe 2011b: 24), because only in the medium of language does the pre-linguistic open up to consciousness and thus to reflection (Meyer-Drawe 2010: 13).

(Written) vignette readings start with specific actions or moments that are perceived and experienced intersubjectively: How are they described? How can they be understood? In the process, the actions of the different participants come into focus (Agostini 2015). The woman has decided – consciously or unconsciously – to 'turn[s] her head slightly to the right'. What would the alternatives have been? With what consequences? The man's gaze remains fixed on the woman for a moment, then he also turns his head to the other side. What does this mean for him? Readings of vignettes raise questions that cannot be answered conclusively but allow for a diversity of perspectives and thus for reflection and expansion. Vignettes do not ask what is – or would have been – 'better', but rather what different experiences reveal and how this can be dealt with from an experiential, and – depending on the interest of the analysis – pedagogical, psychological, sociological or even practical point of view.

Vignette reading is an attempt to understand what happens between people and the world, the perceiver and the perceived. Necessarily, this attempt to reflexively investigate the structures of meaning is not accompanied by simplification but by an increase in complexity (Merleau-Ponty 1976). Not only in vignettes, but also in vignette readings, researchers are on the trail of 'a highly fragile event, namely the moment in which meaning is created' (Meyer-Drawe 2010: 7). The concern of vignette readings is to clothe this genesis of meaning in words and thus to give linguistic expression to the sensuous and bodily expressions that precede any reflection. In vignettes, the meanings of what is perceived are co-constituted through linguistic condensation. This targeted composition and representation directs the focus of perception in the reading towards selected aspects of experience. Although vignettes thus point in a certain direction, their 'vivid density' (Gabriel 2010: 379) generates tangible surpluses of meaning and significance for the reader due to their embodied and pre-reflexive elements. Thus, in the sense of the original meaning of the word *deuten*, vignettes point 'in one direction . . . i.e. but into an open space that can be filled out in different ways' (Gadamer 1967: 10–11). Thus, when we speak of *giving meaning* at this elementary level, it must be understood as a response to the surplus of meaning, the conciseness of what is perceived in the vignette. In vignette readings, the focus is less on giving conclusive answers in the form of explanations, attributions or determinations, but rather on raising questions that invite us to trace the never unambiguous nature of experience.

Reflecting on a vignette hence enables it to be read in all its potential ambiguity. In this context, it reveals and 'points to' (Finlay 2009: 11) the different meanings that can be ascribed to what is perceived. In order to *point to* a possible meaning, something is singled out in the vignette by means of phenomenological 'reduction': what shows up is traced back to the way it shows up (Waldenfels 1992: 30). No interpretations are 'pointed out' here, i.e., no definitive answers or explanations are given that lie 'behind' or 'beyond' what is happening. Instead, there is an attempt to understand the potential of an experience in the course of the event, as it is experienced by the individual. In order to gain a broader viewpoint, experiences and actions can also be considered from a theoretical perspective. Vignette readings look at situations in retrospect, i.e., from a distance, differently, or 'anew' in order to derive knowledge from them.

According to Frederik J. J. Buytendijk, phenomenology is the 'science of examples' (Van Manen 2016: 257). While the writing of a vignette is oriented towards giving examples, the reading of a vignette is oriented towards understanding examples. In the wealth of experience that vignettes outline and articulate, they refer, just like examples, to intersubjective and thus relational experiences that can be intuitively comprehended and therefore recognized. The meaning of a vignette as an example is 'not revealed as an objectification and generalisation of a general rule, but rather arises in intuitive comprehension' (Brinkmann 2012: 44). As a reader, a vignette and the experience it depicts thus give you a particular experience of evidence, in which the phenomenon in question is brought before your eyes. In the process, the peculiar structure of the example transcends its own intention, so that it is shown and you are not told how the example is to be understood.

Buck (1989) has rediscovered the example as a form of the *epagoge*, i.e. Aristotle's technique of 'leading' an individual from the particular to the general: he views it as an important way of understanding and comprehending as well as learning. He undertakes precise analysis of the reflexive 'circular structure' (Buck

1989: 158) of the intuitive process of understanding that the example sets in motion. This reflexive structure opens up contexts of meaning and makes it possible for 'examples . . . to point beyond themselves by pointing back to something' (ibid.: 157). In this way, the specific structure of the example makes it possible for the concrete and particular experience represented in the example to refer to one's own past experiences. At the same time, the example offers the opportunity to gain future knowledge of a multitude of experiences of the same or analogous nature (ibid.: 40). Since the example addresses readers as comprehenders, they must always already have understood the experiential content of vignettes in a certain way. In reading the vignette, this unexpressed, indeterminate and naive experiential knowledge becomes explicit because of their own unreflective expectations and understanding of a particular case, and a general sense becomes explicit. Examples have the intention of making someone think, and thus reify a particular experiential accomplishment. When readers start from their own pre-reflexive experiences, turning back reflexively to their pre-understanding leads them to confront the prior knowledge that has previously been effective in their experiences and in their learning. Because readers have had similar experiences in the past, examples refer them back to those experiences, so that if their expectations are not fulfilled, they can have a new experience that forms the basis for the restructuring of their own prior knowledge about a thing and about themselves as learners – and they themselves learn in the process (Meyer-Drawe 2012b: 15; see also Buck 1989: 80). However, the old experience and its object of knowledge are not simply replaced – as neurobiological discourses in particular might suggest – it is merely their sole validity that is questioned and reindexed. Old opinions and perceptions come to consciousness without being dissolved (Meyer-Drawe 1996: 89).

In contrast to an interpretative, hermeneutic approach to understanding, as envisaged by Buck (1989), by focusing primarily on linguistic acts and written testimonies, phenomenological vignettes take seriously the corporeality of perception that they embody. The experience that is unfamiliar to the reader is not merely seen as a deficit in terms of not yet being understood, it is seen as resistant and indeterminate, eluding radical understanding (Meyer-Drawe 2003: 505). Only in this way is it possible not to assimilate the unfamiliar and the other represented in the vignette and thus merely reconstruct the meaning found within it, but to generate something new and anticipate something that previously did not exist (Brinkmann 2014: 200–3). On the one hand, in the vignette reading researchers distance themselves from the living experiential processes that are described in the vignette by means of concrete actions; on the other hand, it is only in the distance from such processes, through retrospective and perspectivist reflection on the events in question, that a new meaning can be created.

The reflexive and sympathetic comprehension offered by vignette reading of the potential and never fully controllable ambiguity of a text or an experience means that vignettes can be read in very different ways. Phenomenological vignette research aims to respect the particular ways in which experiences are articulated as human and thus makes no claim to objectification or operationalization (Lippitz 2003: 19). Neither is the analysis based on a model or a guided scheme, and comparable categories are not generated. Thus, reading is understood as a 'never-ending process of communicatively structured experiences' (Lippitz 1987: 117). According to Schratz, Schwarz and Westfall-Greiter (2012: 39), the main aim is to 'differentiate the fullness and richness of experiences articulated in them [the vignettes] and to show them in as many facets as possible and in different readings'. In doing so, not everything is included in the reading that reveals itself to the curious reader, but rather a selection is made through 'collecting', 'reading up' or 'compiling' (ibid.: 39–40).

This means that reduction and selection are an unavoidable part of every vignette reading. For the readers, experiences only come into view as very specific phenomena, for example as shame, hope, delight, wonder, awe, excitement, despair, amusement, serenity, remorse, chagrin, uncertainty, frustration, disdain, confidence, failure, eagerness or euphoria. It is this direction of a bodily gaze at the situation from a distance that makes it possible to see certain contexts in the first place, but the gaze is selective and perspective-based; it cannot bring everything into its focus and thus leaves other aspects invisible. However, the vignette always urges readers anew to take a different standpoint when reading within the framework of a horizon, to listen to the calls of an ambiguous world and to find themselves in the process of looking for new experiences.

Example of a vignette reading—Vignette 8: 'Karin and Mr Klotz'

Karin 'should' (must?) perform a piece of music on her accordion for a project before the start of English class. Maybe she sits on a chair away from her usual school desk so that she can find enough space and be heard with her accordion. With most of the attention likely to be focused on her, she starts to play. Before the first note is played, the teacher asks her a question about the structure of the piece of music in a 'sharp tone'. The sharpness of the tone is surprising and makes the listener sit up and take notice. It contrasts with Karin's efforts to play and abruptly interrupts her preparations. Torn from her preparations, Karin responds to Mr Klotz's question. However, her 'shy' answer does not seem to satisfy him. Mr Klotz sternly asks for the form of the song, and Karin, again referring to the sheet of music, gives an answer. Question and answer alternate in a staccato rhythm. The English teacher is obviously taking the opportunity to test the pupil's knowledge of musical forms. Focusing on the sheet of music gives Karin the opportunity to withdraw her gaze from that of the teacher. Nevertheless, she herself remains exposed to the gaze of the others. She can no longer see the stern look he gives his pupil, but she feels it. Is it also a 'standardising gaze' (Foucault 1976: 238) that shines down on the pupil like a spotlight? In any case, this gaze makes her increasingly aware of her own visibility, her exposure to the gaze of others and, not least, her being at the mercy of the teacher's questions.

To be aware of one's visibility, to relate oneself explicitly or inexpressibly to the gaze of others, is peculiarly human. No other living being seems to have ever given itself over to the consideration of how it might appear to others. In his anthropology, Hans Blumenberg (2006) deals decisively with human visibility. Because humans are the only primates to walk upright and no longer have to look downwards, they have excellent vision (ibid.: 777). This breadth of vision, the advantages with which humans were first presented when they changed their habitat from the primeval forest to the savannah, brings with it far-reaching perspectives, especially in the media age. Not only are there no more thickets, foliage or trees to block our view. Looking into the computer or other visual media lets us see much further. But this optimization of visual perception also has a sting. It comes with the risk of increased visibility, because 'this exploded ability to see is . . . at the same time an increased exposure to being seen' (Blumenberg 2006: 777). The benefits of vision are therefore not to be enjoyed without fear. Due to the 'condition of plurality . . . the presence of others who are and act with us' (Arendt 1960: 232), everyone is seen.

The gazes of others who see what Karin herself cannot see imprint themselves on her body (Meyer-Drawe 2000: 117). Do these glances also make her self-conscious and embarrassed? 'The more clearly one recognises the situation, or sees approaching what is perhaps still hidden from others or what they have overheard, the stronger the embarrassment', notes the German philosopher and doctor Hans Lipps (1941: 30). Karin does not answer the teacher's third question; embarrassed, she lowers her eyes to the sheet of music. She probably wants to avoid the eyes of the others. It remains questionable whether Karin no longer knows the answer to the teacher's question or whether she simply does not want to give an answer, wishing to bring this highly emotional situation to a rapid conclusion. Does she perhaps instinctively feel that by giving the wrong answer, i.e. deviating from the teacher's expected answer, this unpleasant situation will only extend even longer in time and space, prompting further (follow-up) questions from the teacher? Her inner tension rises and shows itself in the tight grip with which she now once again holds her accordion. Seeking a hold, she seems to be clinging to it like a drowning woman on a buoy. 'It's called a trio!'; the teacher now gives the answer himself. With a nod, followed by a quiet 'Yes', Karin indicates her agreement. An agreement to what? Is it consent in the sense of thematic agreement or rather an understanding of her own ignorance? In any case, the social positions now seem to have been satisfactorily consolidated. A slight lift of the chin is now more than enough to invite the pupil to perform. At last Karin is allowed to begin. Nervous tension, but also serious effort and concentration, spread across her face.

In the vignette, the gaze is directed very specifically towards the experience of Karin. In the process, 'what appears is traced back to the way it appears' (Waldenfels 1992: 15). Karin's experiences appear differently depending on her location or interests, on her mode of perception and grasp, from close up or from a distance. The composition of the experiences based on the network of actions in the vignette makes material what the researcher has and has not focused on in the educational context. The focus of the gaze frames the experiences and thus first and foremost allows something to appear as something. The fact that something appears as a particular something does not mean that it is something, but that it becomes something in the gaze of the perceiver by receiving – or rather gaining – meaning; this is what allows it to show itself as a particular something in the first place (Waldenfels 2004b: 813–15). Thanks to the conciseness, ambiguity and density of the vignettes, the view can be directed towards often neglected aspects of the teaching and learning process, aspects which often escape the superficial view or even appear superfluous. Yet it is precisely the choreography of the gazes and the bodily movements of the actors in space and time that are able to release a polyphony and deserve a second or even a third look.

Another gaze also descends on Karin. The teacher's gaze has fastened on her face and subjected it to (renewed) scrutiny. No sooner has the last note faded away than his verdict is heard. Does the first, curt 'yes' actually indicate satisfaction? At least he does not seem to have identified any obvious shortcomings during the performance of the piece. 'And look a little angrier when you play,' he adds ironically, perhaps to avoid expressing approval. He then quickly withdraws his gaze from her and with it all his attention. She is no longer worthy of his gaze. 'Take your note books. . .' he orders, addressing the class. In the meantime, Karin leaves her place and quickly lets her accordion disappear from view. She is alone when the blush creeps over her face. Is it the teacher's ironic comment that brings the blush to her cheeks? An implication that means the opposite of what he says, and by which he exposes this apparent weakness of Karin's to the public, precisely by praising it as a strength? Is it a sense of failure, measured against certain standards, that strikes Karin in her very being, causing a sense of shame to stir and making it impossible for her to be with others (Lipps 1941: 30–2)? Shame is 'unavoidable' in learning, as Meyer-Drawe (2013: 96) makes clear: 'For the learner, who must first see through himself as the supposed knower, can be ashamed by this insight. . . . To conclude from this that the path into aporia must be accompanied by the staging of shame is wrong.' Perhaps Mr Klotz deliberately shames Karin, in an attempt to stabilize power and dependency relationships or to discipline his pupil. However, shame, which is what learning is about, cannot be caused by an intentional act (ibid.: 97). Shame is effective: the growing feeling of shame ties

Karin to the present situation and prevents a reflexive distancing from her own self (Rinofner-Kreidl 2009: 157). Like an animal in a cage, she is trapped in a shameful situation. 'The situation, as it is immediately experienced, contains no "offer" of rehabilitation of the self' (ibid.: 168). In this sense, the gazes of others have effectively burned themselves into Karins' body, they have left a 'blind spot' (Waldenfels 2013b: 126), so that she can only see herself through the eyes of these others: 'Now I've disgraced myself,' she says half aloud.

CHAPTER FIVE

Vignette Fields of Application

The applications of vignettes are manifold and this chapter provides you with examples to illustrate their use across a wide variety of academic disciplines in the Global North and the Global South. Based on the phenomenological understanding of experience in which expectations are thwarted and new meanings are generated, vignettes can be created in different contexts and thematic areas: within or outside of lessons at schools, or when experiencing art in a museum, but also as snapshots of social interactions, for example in a train station or on the street.

Hence, vignettes can be written and used:

- in any educational field such as laboratories, sport training, health care, etc.

- in professional education and development.

- in different institutions/work places.

- in the social space: wherever people find themselves, engaging in sport or leisure, in nature, outdoors, homes, etc.

This chapter demonstrates in particular the use of vignettes as professional development and evaluation tools. The focus is on practical applicability, and on providing helpful hints drawn from years of working with vignettes.

Vignettes as professional development tools

The development of the phenomenological vignette as a research tool is closely related to learning in heterogeneous groups in schools. The pioneering project at the University of Innsbruck was followed by other projects in different research fields going beyond the school context. A vignette is a condensed, concise description of a selected scene of experience. It is illustrative in nature and can shed light on the general meaning of specific situations so as to enable learning to take place that will also be of benefit in other experiential situations. Vignettes, therefore, serve as examples and enable researchers to draw general theoretical conclusions from a single specific situation. In addition to the differentiated perception of and reflection on experience that vignettes enable, they also highlight the need for practical action. This means that they can also be used to prompt discussion of implications for practice. Therefore vignettes can also serve as professional development tools (Agostini 2020a, 2020b).

In the international 'ProLernen' project, for example, teaching materials were created with the primary goal of learning to perceive and reflect on experiences in a professional manner (Agostini et al. 2023b).[1] Using vignettes as a training medium enables professionals to focus on alternative ways of perceiving situations, and of thinking and acting in such situations. The aim of vignettes as professional development tools is to nurture a measure of tact in the practice of their work in different professional contexts. Professionalization with vignettes is based on the kind of learning in which all participants are continually ready to challenge familiar and (what they presume are) self-evident points of view through being open to new experiences. Vignettes teach an openness to the surprising and unexpected as these experiences can be both irritating and inspiring, but can lead to new insights. Hence, in order to learn from such reflection on vignettes, particular attention is paid to irritating, surprising and challenging aspects of sensory perception and experience.

Phenomenological professionalization with vignettes is directed at the manner in which one experiences the world before cognitive acts of conceptualization, theorization and abstraction take place. In this context, the focus is not on wanting to change the behaviour of people or solving (their) problems, but rather on gaining a broader perspective on what is happening in a situation and on the people involved. To this end, vignettes aim to teach the need to be attentive to the everyday or quotidian experience, which is not as ordinary as it may seem. They open your eyes to seemingly insignificant moments. These kinds of moments can seem trivial and yet are potentially significant. Work with vignettes and vignette readings, which is at the centre of the approach to professionalization proposed here, is not concerned with categorization or optimization, but with attending to the ambiguous. The focus is on the purposeful observation of situations, as well as listening to and empathizing with those involved in them, in order to understand them in new or different ways and to reflect on what conclusions they enable us to draw with regard to the future. Collective readings of vignettes allow different perspectives through the phenomenological attitude of *epoché* and reduction.

Questions that are the focus of such a professionalization approach are:

1 How can you learn to step back from requirements and situations, in order to be able to look at them anew?

2 What else can a situation tell you when you give specific consideration to corporeality and the associated atmospheres and moods that can impact and affect you?

3 How can you learn to perceive the people who have been entrusted to you, and with whom you have already worked intensively, in such a way that aspects of their potential, problems, strengths and needs that might hitherto have been overlooked or overshadowed come to light and thus become more accessible?

4 And how can you explore new potential approaches or even reflect on and be more aware of the approaches you have used thus far?

Vignettes 14 and 15 were created in the context of the professionalization of (prospective) educators and school leaders within the framework of the 'ProLernen' project. The participants first received an introduction to phenomenological perception (e.g. by means of perception exercises) and corporeality (e.g. by discussing vignettes together in groups and in plenary, with the focus on the corporeality of the people within the vignette). Then they were trained to write vignettes at their workplaces (in this project in schools and nursery schools). The vignettes created were discussed through resonance reading in small groups and revised by the vignette writers. In the process of writing vignettes, 'stumbling blocks' can occur; these are briefly discussed in Box 5.

Box 5 Stumbling blocks

1 *In medias res:* Context should only be presented very briefly at the beginning of the vignette: What contextual information is really necessary to understand the vignette? What does the reader need to be able to imagine the situation?

  1.1. Aim: clarity: e.g. age, gender, distinguishing features or appearance, subject of the lesson, type of exercise, class/grade, location of the organization/work place.

  1.2. What is not necessary (in terms of focus) or has a restrictive effect (as a classification) and thus only allows for one possible interpretation? (e.g. presuppositions or background knowledge of the people in the vignette).

  1.3. Include contextual information in the vignette and do not place it at the beginning (like minutes).

  1.4. Name/introduce all participants in the scene (systematically) from the beginning.

2 Some vignettes can be quite short with a lot of direct speech: What is it really necessary to put into the vignette? Above all, focus on the corporeality, i.e. enrich the raw vignette with facial expressions/gestures.

  2.1. Let gestures/expressions/body postures speak for themselves: What do they look like, for example?

  2.2. Focus on how something becomes perceptible, e.g. how does 'apathetic', 'interested', 'desperate' show up?

3 What is really perceptible? How does it reveal itself? Describe it in such a way as to give a specific impression.

4 If possible, don't use 'because sentences' or 'if-then constructions', for example, 'Then Max realizes that the teacher

won't help him and bangs his fists heavily on his desk in frustration.'

5 Focus less on judgemental/explanatory narration and the meta-perspective. Instead, focus on pre-reflexivity.

6 For longer vignettes, focus on: What exactly irritated/affronted you as a perceiver/writer? What exactly is the experience?

7 Instead of using 'says', 'goes', 'means', 'answers', 'asks'. . . use more descriptive language, i.e. think about *how* he/she is conveying the information. Choose very precise verbs and adjectives (e.g. 'retorts angrily', 'mutters sheepishly', 'solicits imploringly').

8 Be alert to sensations and perception, i.e. also show sounds, smells, cold/warmth, etc.

9 Vignette vs. vignette reading: explanation/*Deutung*/contextualization comes later in the vignette reading.

10 Metaphors and artistic linguistic devices vs. aestheticizing ends in themselves: Please consider very carefully which words you use; they must not serve a solely aesthetic end.

11 Personalize people as much as possible, e.g. not 'Student K.', but 'Karin'; not 'Mr S.', but 'Mr Stein' (anonymized).

12 The vignette writer is not part of the scene (in order not to have to give up his/her attitude of co-experiential experience), unless he/she is directly addressed or unintentionally becomes part of the action. Then he/she enters the vignette in the third person as 'the researcher'.

13 Indicate origin by name or mention it directly, if this is relevant or important for the co-experiential experience.

14 Consciously consider: Who are you giving a name to, and who remains anonymous?

15 Insert the perceived time (if necessary specify the specific duration of an event, e.g. 2 sec., but also show the experience of time, e.g., indicate if it drags on or moves quickly).

16 Give your vignettes neutral titles where possible; more meaningful titles are reserved for vignette readings (e.g. 'Not being heard').

17 Use direct sentences: Instead of 'starts to work', use 'works'; instead of 'starts to open the can', use 'opens the can'; instead of 'starts to speak loudly to the child', use 'speaks'.

18 Tense to use: Present tense.

19 Use gender throughout your vignette.

> **20** Do not insert paragraphs in the vignette, string all the sentences together; it should seem like a scene.
> **21** Lines do not need to be numbered in vignettes.

Vignette 14: 'Vivianne, Dilara and Ms Pilus'

It is stuffy and warm in the classroom, although two windows are wide open. Some of the dark blue curtains are drawn, blocking the view outside. It smells of sausage sandwiches and sweat. Classical music is playing softly on a CD player, the pupils are preparing their crayons as instructed by the teacher, Ms Pilus. Murmurs can be heard. Vivianne opens her pencil case noisily. 'Please start colouring in the picture now. Remember to use different colours for the Easter eggs. They should be nice and colourful. But please don't make the dog green or purple. The faces and hands of the people in the picture are not coloured either. Please colour them in skin colour,' says Ms Pilus. She plucks at her mask and sits down in her chair at the teacher's desk. Vivianne sits next to Dilara. Vivianne starts by colouring the lady's dress in the picture in front of her in a strong dark red. When she has finished, she looks at her work and smiles. She then takes her brown pencil out of the pencil case and colours the lady's face. Dilara looks at her neighbour's work and nudges her. She whispers, 'We are supposed to colour the faces and hands in skin colour, Ms Pilus said. It has to be skin colour.' Dilara shakes her head and holds up a pink crayon, showing it to Vivianne. She turns her gaze to her paper, then looks at her neighbour's picture, which already shows people's faces and hands in pink. Vivianne takes an eraser and tries to erase the brown spots until the sheet tears. She pauses, stares at what is torn, lifts the picture and looks through the coin-sized hole. Almost unconcerned, she puts the sheet down on the table, stands up, goes to the teacher's desk and asks Ms Pilus for a new colouring-in picture.

Vignette writer: Tamara Peer, 2022, Multiplier event on vignette research, University College of Teacher Education Vienna and University of Vienna, Austria, unpublished.

Vignette 15: 'Marvin, Lisa and the second shoe'

The children, already dressed, sit very close together on the narrow cloakroom bench. Marvin – not yet wearing shoes – sits between them with drooping shoulders and a fixed gaze. 'Marvin, you can't go out without shoes,' says teacher Lisa frantically as she glances briefly at him. She is kneeling in front of a girl and buttoning up her jacket. Marvin looks at Lisa, but does not move. After three seconds Lisa calls out in a joyful sounding voice, 'Marvin, please put your shoes on! I know you can do it!' The boy looks down and shakes his head. Then he grumbles, 'No.' Extremely slowly, he finally bends down, pulls a shoe out from behind the bench and holds it out in Lisa's direction. Lisa quickly slides over on her knees, grabs the shoe and slips it onto Marvin's left foot. She accompanies this action with a 'whoosh' and then shouts solemnly, 'Tadahh!' She rests her hands on her thighs and points her head at Marvin's right foot, 'You can put the second one on by yourself.' 'No,' Marvin growls with a serious expression. Lisa and he maintain eye contact. The boy shakes his head. Lisa nods. 'Then no!' he whispers now, shaking his head again. Again Lisa nods, winks at him, shows a sly smile. Marvin shakes his head once more, then a smile flits across his face. Finally he reaches for the second shoe, places it on the floor in front of him and firmly presses his right foot into it. 'A little apart,' Lisa murmurs and pulls the shoe tongue forward. Then Marvin's foot slips into the shoe and with a quick movement of his hand he closes the Velcro fasteners. Lisa smiles, forms her hand into a fist and holds it out to Marvin. He presses his lips together, smiles sheepishly, forms a fist as well and presses it against Lisa's. 'Yeah,' Lisa whispers, turns away and quickly turns back to another child.

> Vignette writer: Theresa Hauck, 2022, Multiplier event on vignette research, University College of Teacher Education Vienna and University of Vienna, Austria, unpublished.

One way of approaching Vignettes 14 and 15 is to read them during a pedagogical or educational conference, or in the context of PLCs, and to analyse them together in the context of a discursive vignette reading. This is not about judging normative evaluations of the teachers', educators' or learners' actions, but about pointing to (*deuten*) the different experiences, perspectives and patterns of meaning. In 'Vivianne, Dilara and Ms Pilus' (Vignette 14) the teacher has given the instruction to paint the faces and hands in 'skin colour'. How did the two girls respond? Which of their own ideas and norms became perceptible? The nursery school teacher in 'Marvin, Lisa and the second shoe' (Vignette 15) has decided – consciously or unconsciously – that Marvin should at least put on the second shoe largely on his own. What is in favour of this? What is against it? What alternatives would there have been? With what consequences? What does this mean for Marvin's learning? How should (nursery school) teachers respond, how can they respond 'tactfully'? How do you think the other students in the class responded to the event of the shoes or the colouring exercise? And why?

The readings of vignettes raise questions which cannot be answered conclusively, but which allow for a diversity of perspectives and thus a reflection and expansion of action. These are aimed at the individual person and their development as well as at the collective. In the joint reading, a mutual and a common understanding with regard to relevant topics can emerge. Or mutual non-understanding becomes manifest and thus can be addressed. This is also where the development of institution comes in, development aimed at achieving a common understanding, which also includes resistance and addresses the whole organization. Vignettes can contribute to an organization's discussion of questions that do not have their starting point in normative ideas, but in concrete experiences of a scene. Vignettes do not pose the question of what is 'better', but what different experiences show and how they can be dealt with. This is deliberately in the plural, as there is no one right way of dealing with it; different alternatives are possible, which can be discussed retrospectively, but have to be rooted in the concrete situation. If we succeed in understanding vignettes as a different way of perceiving experiences, this results in a broadening of perception and understanding for individuals and possibly for the organization as a whole (Agostini and Anderegg 2021).

Vignettes as evaluation tools

In all professional areas and disciplines, it is necessary to check certain work processes, daily routines or activities again and again to see whether they still meet current requirements and expectations. There are numerous approaches to monitoring innovations and developments in various professional disciplines. However, approaches that examine organizational progress and innovation from a phenomenological perspective are less common.

> The need to understand what is going on when an innovation has been tried is essential, as is understanding its impact – in particular before it is scaled up or spread. High-quality tools are needed to yield such data as a basis for decision-making. The vignette model has proven to be a viable alternative for describing without judging and can enable exploration of 'what I think I understand' and help to reveal layers of meaning.
>
> WESTFALL-GREITER and DIENHOFER 2017: 92

We have been asked what added value the use of vignettes (as a data collection tool) brings to the evaluation of innovation and change in the organizational lifeworld. In this regard, Küpers (2015) argues that organizations and their management can be understood as specific lifeworlds from a phenomenological perspective. He sees organizations as an embodied lifeworld of practice, which he describes as follows:

> All organizing processes involve encounters between bodies that derive from or are oriented towards a specific point of seeing, feeling, hearing or touching and acting. The bodies of members of organizations are directed and they take on the shape of this direction, for example, in relation to the what, where and how of the organizing. With an intentional and responsive reflexive approach, what is experienced is not only what is felt or thought; it also opens up various options for relations and action.
>
> KÜPERS 2015: 127

Against this background, vignette research opens up new possibilities for action for those interested in taking a fresh look at the interaction between people and things in the organizational context, in the micro-area of professional action. Vignettes invite you to take a closer look at what is embodied in routine everyday actions. The writing of vignettes makes it possible to see experiences in a way that is not possible in the midst of the events themselves, because you are highly entangled in the situation. Because of the transformational effect of vignette work (see 'Vignettes as a transformative force' section) it is well suited to initiating individual and organizational processes of change and development. These support relearning in professional development, which is a prerequisite for adopting and implementing new procedures. We have selected two organizational areas as examples of the use of vignettes as an evaluation tool.

Application 1: Evaluating organizational encounters

In this section, we illustrate how vignettes can contribute new insights into professional experiences in the organizational lifeworld of embodied practice, enabling consideration of options for further development and relearning. To this end, we present Vignette 16, 'In the examination office'.

Vignette 16: 'In the examination office'

> The head of the examination and study office, Ms Bernstein, appears in the open double door that separates her office from the antechamber. After only one step into the room, she stops at maximum distance from the desk that divides the room, at which the student Suzan is waiting. Ms Bernstein's facial expression is serious, her body straightens. In a determined tone of voice, she addresses the student on the other side of the desk: 'Why do we have deadlines if no one cares about them? As I told you on the phone: I have my rules: if a thesis is not registered and assigned by the Vice Rector, it is not possible to register for the June exam.' Suzan sighs, mentioning misinformation. Ms Bernstein promptly replies, 'The information about deadlines can all be found on the homepage; the deadline was three weeks ago, there's nothing I can do for you.' With a pleading look, Suzan glances around the room, fiddling with two black-bound books with gold engraving, picking up the volumes from the desk, putting them down again, following the contours of her bound work with erratic hands. 'My two young children are sick right now, and I really need to get this degree done before summer.' Her interlocutor repeats

without changing her voice: 'You should have secured the Vice Rector's signature three weeks ago at the very latest. Today is the last day of submission, I'm sorry. The next deadline is in October.' Her tone is determined and monotonous. Ms Bernstein stands erect and motionless, fixing the student with her gaze. Suzan turns to the side, bends her head away from her interlocutor and rolls her eyes. She exhales audibly and loudly, closes her eyes briefly and pauses. After a few seconds, with a jerk, Suzan picks up the two books, holding them tightly against her upper body, adjusts the strap of her shoulder bag, says, 'OK,' quickly turns around, and leaves the room without saying anything else.

> Vignette writer: Norell Flinn,[2] Partial achievement for
> module in master class 2022, Austria, unpublished.

Van Manen suggests two general approaches for gaining deeper insights from the phenomenological reading of a vignette:

1 **Holistic reading:** In this approach, the aim is to capture the overall impression of what happens in the experience described. To this end, the following question is useful: 'How can the . . . original, or phenomenological meaning or main significance of the text as a whole be captured?' (Van Manen 2016: 320). It helps to capture the deep structures of the action in order to avoid superficial interventions, such as blaming the actors for their behaviour. Moreover, the vignette contributes to an enriched understanding of practice in organizations by its programmatic focus on phenomena, things and events in their situatedness and meaning. This involves focusing on the context in which 'all activities and possible praxis' are embedded (Husserl 1970: 142): an embodied nexus of a range of enacted experiences, realized intentions, responsiveness and actions (Küpers 2015: 96).

The multi-sensory description deriving from co-experiential experience strongly conveys the embodiment of the tension between organizational and personal intentions. For Küpers, 'intentions are ambiguous and can be challenged in moments of breakdowns, leading to unintended consequences. Thus, intentions are "in-tensions" in relation to processing and effects' (2015: 131). In our phenomenological approach, this vignette can be used as an evaluation tool to explore individual and organizational responses in the encounter with major disturbances when routine falls short. Accordingly, the encounter depicted in the vignette depicts the clash between institutional norms and subjective need or want that arises in many organizations. Caught in the tension between the *sollen* (what 'should' happen; the intention, purpose and requirements of the organization) and *wollen* (what people 'want': the subjective wishes and needs of the individuals in the organization) of organizational change, professional development has become a significant leadership issue in recent years.

2 **Selective reading:** This approach is more akin to textual analysis, and aims to grasp the phenomenological content of the described experience and its sensory perception from presentation, choice of words and sentence construction, thematic expressions, metaphorical allusions, etc. To this end, Van Manen (2016: 320) suggests the question: 'What statement(s) or phrase(s) seem particularly essential or revealing about the phenomenon or experience being described?'

To answer this question, it has proven useful to first underline, highlight or circle in different colours certain words, parts of sentences or expressive statements that are of importance for specific phenomena. These include words that help express what is shown in the situational co-experiential experience. In Vignette 16, the different positions of the individuals are clearly expressed through different means. With regard to Suzan, for example, there are the following expressions: sighs, glances around with a pleading look, fiddling, picking up and putting down, with erratic hands, bends her head away, rolls her eyes, exhales audibly and loudly, closes her eyes briefly, pauses, turns around. With regard to Ms Bernstein there are formulations such as stops at maximum distance, facial expression is serious, in a determined tone of voice, promptly replies, without changing her voice, determined and monotonous, erect and motionless, fixing with her gaze. The words and phrases quoted carry heavy phenomenological meaning, and some 'phrases that occur in the text may be particularly evocative, or possess a sense of punctum'. (Van Manen 2016: 320).

If the analysis of this vignette is used as an evaluation to initiate professional development, both processes can take place at the organizational and personal levels. Since the situation described in the vignette is obviously a frequent occurrence – as indicated by Ms Bernstein in the text – an organizational development process could be initiated in response, which attempts to address this dilemma at institutional level. Organizational action is characterized by external and internal requirements, which are adopted by the actors concerned in various ways and become guiding principles for their actions. These requirements can take the form of regulations and standards, but can also be introduced as the results of internal processes. The extent to which they are actually considered by the actors in the organization depends to a large extent on their identification with them and how they are then put into practice. At the individual level, the vignette can be used in the relevant phase of the study program to confront students with the consequences they will face if they do not submit their final theses on time. In contrast to a conventional information notice, Vignette 16 triggers a much more impactful bodily response as it is felt from within the embodied situation experienced by Suzan.

Application 2: Evaluating facets of leadership

In management literature, there is now an unmanageable number of publications on the understanding of leadership, which makes it difficult to navigate the jungle of information. Entering 'leadership' into a search engine on the Internet results in 4,830,000,000+ hits. Nevertheless – or perhaps precisely because of this – the well-known American leadership researcher Warren Bennis (McGregor 2014) comes to the conclusion, 'To an extent, leadership is like beauty: It's hard to define but you know it when you see it.' This statement is an indication that the many facets (Cannon 2009) and nuances (Fullan 2019) of leadership can only be revealed in experiences in an organizational context.

Against the background of the empirically unclear starting point, a research group at the University of Innsbruck was invited by the Robert Bosch Foundation, Germany, to explore what constitutes success for school leaders in terms of educational processes and results. To answer this question, the members of the research group travelled to twenty-eight schools that had received the German School Award to experience on site how the manifold facets of school leadership revealed themselves (Schratz et al. 2022).[3] To capture these experiences phenomenologically, they also wrote vignettes during their stay, selecting particular moments from their co-experiential experience. For Markus Ammann, a member of the research group, 'vignettes offer the potential to make leadership experiences visible to others. Vignettes thus open up a new, supplementary perspective not previously available to researchers, in which the traces that leadership practices have left on school participants are revealed' (2018: 10). Vignette 17 'My super friend' is an example from the fieldwork.

Vignette 17: 'My super friend'

> On the first tour of the elementary school that the principal takes with the researcher, children keep running toward them, greeting Mr Whitehead, the principal and passing by. Mark, another boy, stops abruptly, and raises his right hand palm up toward Mr Whitehead. The principal perceives it, his face lights up. Clapping his palm, he looks into his eyes and curiously asks 'Sad?' 'Nope, just gotta go to the bathroom!' bounces back from Mark. Around the next corner, another student rushes toward him and lunges at him, wrapping his arms around him as if he was hugging a tree. Eyeing the astonished guest, he says in a clear tone of voice, 'He's not my friend, he's my super friend!'
>
> SCHLEY and SCHRATZ 2021: 97–8

In the evaluation of a particular situation in an organizational context, it is of great benefit to engage collectively with the vignette. If a group works together as a PLC its members can draw lessons for their future professional development from the transformational experience of using vignettes as evaluation tools. In addition to the evaluative questions for vignettes already presented by Van Manen, the four approaches presented in Box 6 (from Schratz, Schwarz and Westfall-Greiter 2012: 51–4) are useful when discussing vignettes' phenomenological embodiment of experiences in the larger context.

Box 6 Four approaches to discussion

Approach 1: 'Leadership as . . .'

1 Read the vignette and let it sink in.
   - What is happening here?
   - What kind of experience is revealed in this vignette?
   - What does the atmosphere feel like?
   - What resonances and/or irritations do I feel?

2 In the group:
   - How does leadership show up in this vignette?
   - Complete the sentence, 'Leadership (shows itself) as . . .' with verbs to explore the concept of leadership.

3 Dialogue:
   - What do these insights into leadership mean for us in practice?
   - How can we further extend our understanding of leadership?

Approach 2: Different lenses

1 In the group, consider which lenses individuals wish to use to read this vignette: the perspective of the child, the school leader, the researcher.

2 Read the vignette and let it resonate with you.
   - What resonances and/or irritations do you sense?
   - Underline words and phrases that are particularly meaningful to you, which show the essence of the experience.
   - What themes do you recognize?

3 Dialogue:
   - What did we notice when looking through our respective lenses? What comes to mind?
   - How do the individual perspectives combine to form an overall impression?

Approach 3: Deep reading

1 Read the vignette and let it have an effect on you.
   - What resonances and/or irritations do you feel?
   - What is revealed here?

2 In the group:
'Read the vignette sentence by sentence'. 'After each sentence, allow group members to ask questions about the sentence'.
'When the questions run out, move on to the next sentence'.

3 Dialogue:
– What has been revealed in the questions?
– How did the vignette gain clarity? What remains obscure?

Approach 4: Reading for writing

1 Read the vignette and let it affect you. Then do some freewriting to release and capture your thoughts and reactions.[4] Write non-stop for three to five minutes. If nothing comes to mind, bridge the silence with words about the flow of writing, for instance, '. . . nothing there and waiting to . . . blah blah blah . . .' until a new thought finds the writing hand and leads it on.

2 In the group, share your impressions using the active listening method: each member reads their freewriting aloud or describes the impressions that occurred to them while writing. Group members listen. No discussion!

3 Dialogue:
– What do we have in common? How do the readings differ?
– What seems essential to us here?
– What does this mean for our own practice?

We invite you to try out some of these approaches yourself on a vignette you have created, or on one of the many vignettes collected in this book, and to gain experience with them in a group. Both the creation of a vignette from co-experiential experience and phenomenologically oriented readings need to be practised like any other research instruments in order to enable them to be used to their full potential. Check specific sections of this book if you need further support or background information.

CHAPTER SIX

Vignette Research as a Human Experience

The vignette research presented in this book has opened up new directions for research. Researchers and practitioners in different parts of the world have shared their experience that vignette research has led to new ways of thinking, opened up new possibilities for action and given them a new sense of direction. When we have worked with people from different professions and scientific backgrounds, they have always experienced vignette research as a social process that concerns them – and does something to them. Some participants even reported that they gained authority and strength from the experience of writing. Dealing with more abstract data does not usually provide the researcher with such an immediate response and is more informative than performative. The approach we have taken in this book concerns a particular form of research which includes rather than excludes human experiences in researching everyday social situations. In contrast to the globalization of data collection, vignette research concentrates on the lifeworld of individuals and how they engage with the world and its objects in their everyday lives. This chapter is therefore devoted to the implications of the multilayered nature of human relationships within the experience of vignette research.

Treating perceptions and feelings seriously

Those involved in vignette research have also shared some challenges, particularly when they felt that the role of the researcher (as a participant or observer) was becoming somewhat blurred. When joining the research community, most had been familiarized with the criteria of objectivity, validity and reliability and had been socialized to distance themselves from the immediacy of sensory experience in order to keep control of the data gathering process. However, in any human experience '[s]ynaesthetic perception is the rule, and we are unaware of it only because scientific knowledge shifts the center of gravity of experience, so that we have unlearned how to see, hear, and generally speaking feel, in order to deduce, from our bodily organization and the world as the physicist conceives it, what we are to see, hear and feel' (Merleau-Ponty 2009: 266). The paradox is that research that starts from a position of treating people's perceptions and feelings seriously may find itself creating situations in which these same perceptions and feelings are threatened with erasure (Schratz and Walker 1995: 38).

The visible and the invisible

The prevailing research culture has a lot to do with words and numbers and other symbolic representations of knowledge and seldom relies on the fact that the socialization of every human being's cognition actually begins in early childhood with quite different modes of access and acquisition, namely seeing, hearing, smelling, tasting, touching, acting – precisely with physical and sensory activities (Piaget and Inhelder 1969). At the latest, by the time children start school, images and text form large parts of their world, although we have long known that the extent to which such symbolic representation can replace or even extend original experience is severely limited (Bruner and Olson 1978: 312).

The symbolism of words, numbers and other operators determines our everyday life: we read newspapers and books to gain information, in times of rapidly growing digitalization not only on paper, but increasingly on different media. Alongside numeracy, literacy is the cornerstone of every compulsory curriculum, and the education system of which it is a part is put to the test worldwide via the Programme for International Student Assessment (PISA) (Schleicher 2018). Behind the visibility of every written text is an invisible world of experiences that a person has had since entering the world: encounters with thousands of other individuals from family members to peers, teachers and various fellow citizens in private and professional life. These diverse experiences form the subjective filter through which we experience the world, which cannot be transferred or reconstructed.

For a variety of reasons, scientists are sometimes regarded as 'distant' and experienced as being detached from the actual problems of people's everyday lives. During the COVID-19 pandemic in particular, it became apparent from the perspective of society as a whole that the sometimes controversial debate among scientists led to uncertainty among many people, since scientists' judgements were often not transparent and comprehensible. Research data were presented in a brittle manner and detached from the world of experience, which meant that they could not connect to people's experience. Since these original experiences are hidden behind statistical averages or only appear as 'outliers' diverging from a statistical average, it is important that scientists, at least when communicating their findings, align themselves with the lives and needs of the people they are addressing. In this case it makes sense to

> take a standpoint that is different from that of the external and objective observer. We need to find a form that places the authors inside events, and allows the reader access to the writers. We also need a form that disrupts the expectation that theory and practice are discrete and separable and that the gap between cognition and affect can be kept water-tight and heavily insulated.
>
> SCHRATZ AND WALKER 1995: 15–16

Fritz Breithaupt, whose research is in human communications, points out that narratives help to make the world comprehensible. 'Narratives help us order the information that comes at us. People develop an attitude toward the issues of the world when they find themselves emotionally in a narrative – but not when they read a list of ten abstract arguments and bullet points' (Breithaupt 2022: 36). Vignette research represents the micro-perspective of a narrative that does not simplify complexity, but rather focuses on the 'thicket of the lifeworld' (Matthiesen 1985) and presents a narrative of co-experiential experience. Personal feedback from participants in vignette work such as 'This makes me feel understood' points in this direction.

The interrelationship between cognition and emotion

'Feelings have a hard time in modernity. Everyone knows they exist, but how do they exist and where? Evaluation fluctuates between disparagement and exuberance,' writes Waldenfels (2004b: 27). Cognition and emotion are usually divided into separate worlds in scientific research. In the co-experiential experience of everyday encounters, cognition and emotion are inseparably linked and perceived holistically. In order for this holistic co-experiential experience to be expressed, it is important to develop a convincing way of writing vignettes. Since vignette writers only have language at their disposal, they have to make effective use of words, syntax and style to depict as much as possible of the uniqueness of human encounter(s). This is crucial to creating an effect on the reader that mirrors the researcher's co-experiential experience.

Vignette research is confronted with the following dilemma: we have (only) language at our disposal when we want to convey experiences that are based on everyday encounters. The language we use to do so is limiting, not only in terms of the letters, words and grammatical constructions that are available to us, but also in our learned ability to use language as a means of expression. This ability is further refined after schooling through professional socialization, which is expressed in the different types of texts produced by, for example, a lawyer, a scientist or a writer. In our workshops, we encountered these different writing socializations again and again. Participation in freewriting classes has proven helpful when inhibitions or blockages have arisen in the writing process.

We illustrate the interrelationship between cognition and emotion in Figure 7, with the iceberg model. The only visible features of the vignette text are represented by the choice of words, the composition of the text, etc. As visible characters on paper or in digitized form, they form the tip of the iceberg (the visible). The

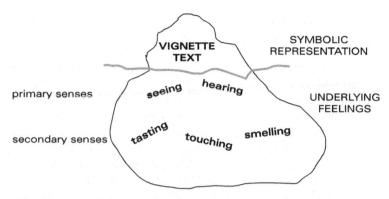

FIGURE 7 *Iceberg model of the emotional world.*
Source: Authors

deeper dimensions can only be hinted at because they are below the waterline in the iceberg model and are thus not visible.

Figure 7 illustrates the challenge we face in vignette research. Our expertise builds on all the skills we have previously acquired in order to meet personal and professional challenges. In applying the phenomenological *epoché*, we need to bracket the prior knowledge that helps us understand a situation in everyday life. The suspension of the known should lead to an 'attitude of emphatic curiosity and exploratory openness' (Küpers 2015: 102) and thus use all the embodied senses beneath the surface of the water in Figure 7. If we only rely on what we see, we restrict our experiential capacity to perceiving the visible part of the iceberg. This is like watching a silent movie. If we include the perception of the senses, we can listen to what people are communicating and can feel the atmosphere. (As per the experience recorded in Vignette 6, 'Moving people', we are confronted with the situation that silence is also a sound we have to be aware of!)

Seeing and hearing are the primary senses used by vignette writers. Secondary senses such as smell, taste and touch arise less often. It is only with visually impaired people that we have found these senses to come more strongly to the fore. Beyond the five senses that determine our perception of the external world, there are sensory perceptions such as pain, hunger, thirst, etc., all of which are embodied in human action. However, these sensory perceptions do not occur in isolation in everyday life, but are intertwined with the body, an experience described in the literature as synaesthesia.

Individual researchers refer to a form of 'sensory slippage' to address this intersensory experience.

> Our sensuality and sensibility are the fertile, though contingent 'ground' of our temporally relative being-in-the-world. We not only have our own intelligibility (Lingis 1996), but also relate to sensory materialities and expose ourselves in a sensuous mediality of luminosity, tactility and sonority. . . . Importantly, our experiences, as senses, are multi-sensory and synesthetic, allowing us i-n-t-e-r-modal perception. Synaesthesia is usually described as a form of sensory slippage (Baron-Cohen and Harrison 1997), by which sensory experience with one modality involuntarily triggers percepts in another. However, in a non-clinical sense, synaesthesia is an alternative way of considering sensoriality. This alternative implies that one sense evokes another, which in turn can evoke further senses; there are thus i-n-t-e-r-sensorial links within the body and synaesthesia engages with the everyday objects the world and in our everyday lives.
>
> KÜPERS 2015: 116

The interplay between agency and structure

However, vignette research also has a political dimension. As a *zoon politikon*, humans are social and political beings who are connected to a community, but also want to have influence and a say (Arendt 1960). This dimension also becomes apparent in vignette research, as the interplay of agency and structure is manifest in every social encounter. Culturally embedded human habits influence how people think and act in social situations. 'These habitual ways of thinking and acting become embedded over time in the social structures we enact, but alternative social structures can also be created' (Scharmer 2007: xiii). In his structuration theory, Anthony Giddens (1984) 'talks of the duality of structure in which social structures are not fixed sets of rules and resources but are features of social systems that have to be recreated in the specific moment of action. Such recreation can only take place when human agents act in this way or that and a powerful influence at that point is the reflexivity and knowledgeability' (Frost 2006: 4). The implication of Giddens's theory of action is therefore that social or organizational structures can be modified by the agency of individuals.

In its transformational impact, vignette research offers a promising opportunity to deal with the interplay between agency and structure and opens up new ways of thinking and acting. Depending on its application, the resonance reading phase can be utilized to consider different perspectives: sometimes the perspective of agency comes more to the fore in the actions of those involved, sometimes the structural impediments in the situation are more important. Since the co-experiential experience is the underlying foundation of the vignette, it is not only the participants in the vignette who are discussed, but also the vignette researchers themselves. It is worth looking at the blind spots of individual researchers or the collective blind spots within PLCs when working on the interplay between agency and structure.

Implementing this kind of pedagogy is easier said than done in practice, because it embraces the complex, entangled nature of what Laing describes in his social phenomenology as 'inter-experience', the relation between my experience of you (i.e. 'you-as-I-experience-you') and your experience of me ('me-as-you-experience-me') (1967: 15–16). Vignettes depict inter-experience because the researchers intentionally experience others as experiencing. Let us take the school environment, in which vignette research has its origins. When teachers read a vignette, they experience classroom interactions between teachers and students. This inter-experience helps them to become mindful of the learning experience in a way that is not theoretical or abstract and therefore resists reconciliation or alignment with their own past and future teaching experiences. The students' experiences become a learning experience for the teachers. They are indirectly taught about their own teaching experience through the experiences of students (Schratz, Schwarz and Westfall-Greiter 2013).

However, working with professionals (here: teachers) involves a challenge: as professional educators they might believe that their own education is complete and might

> try to impose a taken-for-granted set of beliefs and values. Inevitably such 'education' turns into a pedagogy of oppression – an authoritarian form of domination of adults over children.

The 'completed' educator tends to see children as incomplete. No need then to listen to children. Impossible to learn from them.

VAN MANEN 1986: 15

Our concluding thought is to point out again that vignette research is a human experience with all the fallacies of human life. We cannot dispose of these fallacies, but we can strive for a professional ethos that humanity has been familiar with from ancient times. The awareness of our humanity shows itself as 'good' and a 'successful practice', in which a person positions himself or herself on the basis of ethical values and professional experience, and takes responsibility. Rather than creating clinical research conditions to exclude the deviations that result from the researcher and the environment, vignette researchers use all their senses to grasp the uniqueness and density of lifeworld experiences. In such situations, Merleau-Ponty (2009) argues that human beings' senses interact, evoking and involving each other, overlapping, blurring, segueing and transgressing. In everyday fieldwork, it is the sense of things that keeps the research encounter responsive. Therefore, in vignette writing, situating yourself beside a human being is a very personal act. Be aware of the fragility of responsivity.

CHAPTER SEVEN

The Way Forward

Now that you have learned about the scientific foundations of vignette research and its different areas of application, you have an innovative tool at your disposal with which to explore your own research queries. Questions may emerge such as: Where do we go from here? What further contexts or topics can be opened up through vignette research or integrated into it? This concluding and forward-looking chapter raises the issue of the interdisciplinarity of research, the question of multilingual contexts and inclusive education, but also the well-being and the future of education and research, concluding that vignette research opens up opportunities and broadens perspectives, but that it also has limitations and poses challenges.

Interdisciplinary research

Globally there are increasing drives to support, encourage, build and develop interdisciplinary research in order to solve the challenges with which society is confronted today. Universities around the world are putting support structures in place that will increasingly allow researchers to work in interdisciplinary teams. In many ways, interdisciplinary research has already been conducted for several decades. It has certainly provided avenues for richer research insights to emerge, and for creative and innovative solutions to be explored with regard to phenomena ranging, for example, from classroom practices to the utilization of public spaces to architecture to health education and communication systems.

Interdisciplinary research is a very powerful vehicle that enables us to respond to the challenges facing society. Specifically, in terms of the broader agenda for a better world, Agenda 2030, interdisciplinary research is not only encouraged, it is absolutely critical to support sustainability and more specifically the seventeen SDGs. The SDGs address key issues for creating a peaceful, prosperous and sustainable planet for future generations. However, the SDGs are interconnected and demand interdisciplinary research. Vignette research provides an ideal vehicle for building bridges between different disciplines in the science community. In specific sciences or in specific disciplines, certain research methodologies often predominate. As a fairly new and innovative research methodology, vignette research provides an avenue through which bridges can be built to strengthen interdisciplinary research even further in the future.

Multilingual contexts

Multilingual contexts, specifically in education, have been a point of discussion for many years. With high levels of global mobility, mass migrations and population moves between continents, countries and across national borders, our schools and classrooms are becoming increasingly multilingual. Even within countries and between regions, migrations are continuously taking place. Work environments are increasingly global, and transnational companies mean that the workforce is often linguistically diverse. Vignettes provide a compelling way to create rich knowledge in a variety of the world's languages.

Science and scientific findings are often captured within dominant world languages. Vignettes provide the opportunity for minority languages to also come to the fore and contribute to specific insights within a variety of scientific fields. Therefore, in terms of utility, vignettes are a very appropriate research methodology within multilingual contexts.

Inclusive education

Methodological approaches can reach their limits in the context of diversity, and can face the demand to address the issues and needs of all users. Vignette research requires an attitude in which all the human senses are involved: not only the sense of sight, but also the sense of smell, touch and hearing. This can become a challenge for some researchers in that their senses are limited. At the same time, we are currently testing vignette research with researchers who cannot see, for example. What is becoming clear in these vignettes – as in other vignettes written by people without visual impairment – is that certain senses predominate, e.g. the sense of sight is very prominent in sighted people. In the vignette of a blind researcher, however, noises, sounds and smells have a strong influence. Different people each give preference to different modes of perception. Successful vignettes manage to bring to life a scene full of sounds, noises, impressions and auditory experiences. However, it is also possible to give preference to certain senses and still recreate a scene.

Particularly with regard to inclusion, it is also essential to be aware that perceptions are influenced by group and category, and have an understanding of what constitutes normality (for example, see Vignette 14, 'Vivianne, Dilara and Ms Pilus', in the 'Vignettes as professional development tools' section). Prior experiences thus have an exclusionary and limiting character, and the knowledge of this can enhance your understanding of differences that arise in supposedly homogeneous groups, for example, affecting the perception of participants and their experiences. Bracketing and refraining from judgement can offer a way of engaging with diversity. For this, it is essential to maintain an open attitude towards perception (Peterlini 2019).

However, in their specificity and ambiguity, vignettes allow researchers different, partly disparate perceptions of and approaches to meaning, which can be reflected in the diversity of the lifeworld and through joint exchange in a group. In the simultaneous experience of indeterminacy and the productive creation of meaning, difference and equal perspectives, the potential of appreciating what can be perceived concretely but not captured propositionally or conceptually is also high. Vignettes often make the unfamiliar material in order to point out (alternative) possibilities; they undermine one's own framework of attitudes and expectations because they elude one-dimensional definitions. At the same time, they open up new perspectives going beyond our usual patterns of perception. Therein lies an inclusive potential. Where well-trodden paths no longer lead anywhere, other possibilities beyond those we have prepared for must come into view. This requires an open-minded attitude and attention to others and the world, an attitude that can come into play unexpectedly in the encounter with vignettes. The nuances of inclusive education that can be captured through vignette research are illustrated by Vignette 18 and Schwarz's discussion of 'Sebastian'.

The first encounter with Sebastian took place in the field, during the initial research visit; the sociopolitical background was a pilot reform programme in Austrian schools, establishing middle schools for 10-to-14-year-olds. After arriving in the small, fog-shrouded community, I walked to the school, which, surrounded by the village museum, corner shop, church and parish building, underwent substantial renovation both educationally and architecturally during the subsequent research visits. The location was symptomatic of the school: for the headmaster, being in the village centre meant that the teachers saw themselves as embedded in village life and were also expected to get involved in it. What followed were initial contacts with the school management, colleagues, while the bulletin board announced my research visit to the school. Mathematics was the first lesson to which a colleague took me, and in which the following vignette took place in the form of a first encounter with Sebastian and his learning process.

Vignette 18: 'Sebastian'

> Sebastian is busy transferring the mathematical content of an index card into his booklet.
>
> –'What are you doing there?'
> – 'I am taking this down'
> – 'Is this helping you study mathematics?'
> – 'Nope!' This comes back as if shot out of a pistol.
> – 'What would help you?'
> – 'A calculator!'
>
> > Vignette writer: Johanna F. Schwarz, 'Entering the field, making contact, setting the scene', September 2010, West Austria, unpublished.

The immediacy with which Sebastian denigrates the task he is given is not only a particular trait of vignette writing, it also sheds a light on the relation that forms the basis of this kind of research. Does Sebastian seem to view the task he has to complete more as a writing task than a calculation? Does he regard working with the index card as an unnecessary detour in comparison to the pocket calculator? Which would deliver the result quicker?

'He is a character, a minimalist!' This explicit statement, made by one teacher in my presence, irritates me, makes me think and lays the foundation for my extensive research on the phenomenon of attribution. What speaks to us in the research situation, what catches our eye, what startles us and makes us wonder is exactly what should guide us as vignette researchers when endeavouring to co-experientially experience what students and teachers experience in schools. The attitude we adopt when crafting what we co-experientially experience in vignettes is what we call an engaged perspective. Questions such as the following take centre stage: What kind of impact does such a statement have on Sebastian when he does not even hear it, how does it exert its power, how does it inscribe itself into his body, how does it become ascertainable and describable? Sebastian has a striking appearance. He is of small, almost girlish stature, he seems shy and reserved, if not withdrawn, and has striking physical tics that challenge most of the teachers on the team: a facial twitch and a barely perceptible pointing with his index finger at the chin of his face when he asks for permission to speak. When he does so his voice is firm and loud and clear, making the disparity between the characteristics ascribed to him and his outer appearance even more surprising. Conversations with students and teachers in the field as part of the reading of (rough) vignettes – another central step in vignette research – allow such striking insights to emerge, and reveal that students often experience learning and lessons in a very different way than teachers have planned.

Even in the first few minutes of our presence in the field, while waiting with the students for the school doors to open, we are greeted by a wealth of experiences in any school we visit. In order to see this, it is vital, however, that we regard schools as unfamiliar terrain. We have been in such environments during the formative years of our life, and so we tend to believe we know exactly what is going on in schools – even more so if we are teacher educators or school researchers. Vignette researchers aim to set aside our previous knowledge, that is, to not assume we know what will unfold before us when we step through the school doors. We adopt the stance of strangers to the field, seeking respectful rapprochement and demonstrating the willingness to enter a shared pedagogical space. Sebastian eventually showed himself to be a gifted natural scientist and number cruncher in the course of my time with him in the field. Vignettes are exemplary in nature, and when telling their stories a particularly sensitive stance is recommended – a feel for the small gesture, the poignant look, the tone of what is being said, the hidden gift.

Well-being

There has been a global movement towards a deeper understanding of well-being, and also towards prioritizing it. Whether the focus is hedonic or eudaimonic well-being, the research community has seen an explosion of well-being studies across a range of disciplines. While well-being studies generally originated in psychology, the topic is now also being explored in fields such as economics, statistics, business studies, leadership sciences, theology, health sciences and even finance.

Vignette research can capture the nuances within well-being research where it is often difficult to measure the subjective construct itself. While there are statistical and psychometric measures with which well-being can be assessed, vignette research offers the opportunity to understand the uniqueness of well-being within an individual, personal experience (Eloff et al. 2023). It also offers the opportunity to track well-being experiences across time to ensure that well-being research is not viewed as a static concept. Vignette research has substantial potential within the broader domain of well-being research due to its focus on co-experiential experience.

Future of education and research

How can we rethink research and education in order to shape the future? Education and research can help us to reimagine a world of increasing complexity, uncertainty and precarity. Global challenges such as pandemics, accelerated climate change, persistent inequalities, social fragmentation, and political extremism, and also digital innovations such as artificial intelligence and biotechnology, are compelling people to ask fundamental questions about their place in the world and the many ways they rely on one another. Such challenges make people question their relationship with the world, themselves and others in order to reassess how differentiation and exclusion impacts on lives, lifeworlds and horizons. In this context, vignette research can shed new light on social bonds, and shared vulnerabilities and responsibilities.

Learning with vignettes can strengthen humans' sense of duty towards each other. Such duty seems clear when those in need are close to the researchers, both physically and in terms of the senses; it is less clear when they are more distant. The underlying principle of vignette research is a sense of responsibility that does not originate from one's own initiative and that is already evident in researchers when they pay attention to others or allow themselves to be irritated by them. This responsibility, understood as sensitivity to the vulnerability of the unfamiliar and the other, also finds its way into vignettes. As literary texts, they challenge and irritate their readers, imposing a sensory, bodily responsibility on them. In responding to the narratively condensed experiences in the vignettes, in relating to them, a form of responsive ethics comes into play that predates any sense of 'right' or 'wrong'.

In this context of responsive ethics, the responding attention of the researcher begins with this unfamiliar claim, the perception of which merges with the obligation it brings. This appeals to researchers' bodily vulnerability and ethical concerns and is rooted in both sensory responsiveness (Lévinas 1992: 274) and non-indifference (Waldenfels 1994: 556–7). With vignettes, researchers enter into the situation that has been depicted, reading about it and retracing it, and where appropriate acting it out, empathizing with the description, exploring what can be learned from it for the future. The goal is to highlight the range of experiences, perspectives and possible meanings, bringing them into the open and enabling them to be worked with.

NOTES

Chapter 1

1 Michael Schratz, Johanna F. Schwarz and Tanja Westfall-Greiter initiated a research project that was financially supported by the Austrian Science Fund (FWF) under grant No. P 22230-G17.

2 In vignettes names are always anonymized. We have also applied this rule in this introductory vignette.

3 Throughout the book, texts and vignettes from non-English texts by cited authors have been translated by the authors and corrected by the translators of this book. In some instances, even when a published English translation was available for an author, the non-English text was still consulted in order to capture the original intent.

4 In a survey, 'a vignette can be a one-sentence description of a hypothetical situation, where the respondent is asked to make a choice between two alternatives about what "ought" to happen' (Finch 1987: 107) and where only a limited number of circumstances are to be explored. However, vignettes can be made more complex, specifying the features of each situation in detail. This makes the question the respondent has to answer more concrete and focused on specific circumstances. In addition, open-ended questions can be inserted (Finch 1987).

5 Our thanks to Käte Meyer-Drawe for providing us with valuable information on the use of vignettes in other fields of research.

6 'Investigator bias' refers to a subtle or unconscious behaviour of the researcher towards an expected result.

Chapter 2

1 Minor linguistic adaptations were made to the vignette after its initial publication in English.

2 Minor linguistic adaptations were made to the vignette after its initial publication in English.

Chapter 3

1   The direct quote from the participant is from the raw data and has therefore not been revised to correct the English.

Chapter 5

1   The *ProLernen – Professionalisation of educators and educational leaders through learning research with vignettes –* project was funded by the Erasmus+ program/2020-1-AT01-KA203-077981 (11/2020-11/2022).
2   Name changed at the request of the author.
3   Robert Bosch Stiftung, 'German School Award', accessed 11 July 2023.
4   *Freewriting* is a method of creative writing in which the writer's stream of consciousness is put down on paper without reflection, evaluation, or attempts to come up with suitable formulations. Sentences, sentence fragments, and individual words emerge from a continuous flow of writing.

REFERENCES

Agostini, E. (2015), 'The Many Facets of "Creating": A Phenomenological Investigation of "Creating" in the Learning Process', *Procedia – Social and Behavioral Sciences*, 191: 2494–9.

Agostini, E. (2016a), *Lernen im Spannungsfeld von Finden und Erfinden: Zur schöpferischen Genese von Sinn im Vollzug der Erfahrung*, Paderborn: Schöningh.

Agostini, E. (2016b), 'Lektüre von Vignetten: Reflexive Zugriffe auf Erfahrungsvollzüge des Lernens', in S. Baur and H. K. Peterlini (eds), *An der Seite des Lernens: Erfahrungsprotokolle aus dem Unterricht an Südtiroler Schulen – ein Forschungsbericht. Mit einem Vorwort von Käte Meyer-Drawe und einem Nachwort von Michael Schratz. Gastbeiträge von Dietmar Larcher und Stefanie Risse. Erfahrungsorientierte Bildungsforschung*, Vol. 2, 55–62, Innsbruck: StudienVerlag.

Agostini, E. (2017), 'Lernen, neu und anders wahrzunehmen: Vignetten und Lektüren – Formen professionsbezogener (ästhetischer) Bildung?', in M. Ammann, T. Westfall-Greiter and M. Schratz (eds), *Erfahrungen deuten – Deutungen erfahren: Experiential Vignettes and Anecdotes as Research, Evaluation and Mentoring Tool. Erfahrungsorientierte Bildungsforschung*, Vol. 3, 23–38, Innsbruck: StudienVerlag.

Agostini, E. (2019), 'Zur Verdichtung und Analyse von Unterrichtsvignetten', *Journal für LehrerInnenbildung*, 19 (4): 92–101.

Agostini, E. (2020a), 'Lernen "am Fall" versus Lernen "am Beispiel". Oder: Zur Bedeutung der pathischen Struktur ästhetischer Wahrnehmung für die Narration von phänomenologisch orientierten Vignetten', in H. K. Peterlini, I. Cennamo and J. Donlic (eds), *Wahrnehmung als pädagogische Übung: Theoretische und praxisorientierte Auslotungen der phänomenologisch orientierten Bildungsforschung. Erfahrungsorientierte Bildungsforschung*, Vol. 7, 153–78, Innsbruck: StudienVerlag.

Agostini, E. (2020b), *Aisthesis – Pathos –Ethos: Zur Heranbildung einer pädagogischen Achtsamkeit und Zuwendung im professionellen Lehrer/-innenhandeln Erfahrungsorientierte Bildungsforschung*, Vol. 6, Innsbruck: StudienVerlag.

Agostini, E. (2022), 'Notes on Doing Vignette Research', Personal communication, 26 February 2022.

Agostini, E. and N. Anderegg (2021), '"Den Zauber von Unterricht erfassen": Die Arbeit mit Vignetten als Beitrag zur Professionalisierung und Schulentwicklung', *Lernende Schule – Für die Praxis pädagogischer Schulentwicklung*, 94 (24): 26–9.

Agostini, E., N. Öztürk, S. Prummer, V. Schatz, V. Symeonidis and A. Thielmann (2023a), 'Vignette: The Vignette as a Tool for Reflection, in E. Agostini, H. K. Peterlini, J. Donlic, V. Kumpusch, D. Lehner and I. Sandner (eds), *The Vignette as an Exercise in Perception: On the Professionalisation of Educational Practices*, 36–44, Leverkusen-Opladen: Barbara Budrich.

Agostini, E. and H. K. Peterlini (2023), 'Vignette Research: An Austrian Phenomenological Approach to Empirical Research', in T. Feldges (ed.), *Education in Europe: Contemporary Approaches across the Continent*, 130–40, London: Routledge.

Agostini, E., H. K. Peterlini, J. Donlic, V. Kumpusch, D. Lehner and I. Sandner, eds (2023b), *The Vignette as an Exercise in Perception: On the Professionalisation of Educational Practice*, Leverkusen-Opladen: Barbara Budrich.

Agostini, E., H. K. Peterlini and M. Schratz (2019), 'Pädagogik der Leiblichkeit? Phänomenologische und praxistheoretische Perspektiven auf leibliche Erfahrungsvollzüge in Schule und Unterricht', in M. Brinkmann, J. Türstig and M. Weber-Spanknebel (eds), *Leib – Leiblichkeit – Embodiment: Pädagogische Perspektiven auf eine Phänomenologie des Leibes Phänomenologische Erziehungswissenschaft*, Vol. 8, 197–226, Wiesbaden: VS Verlag für Sozialwissenschaften.

Aguiar de Sousa, L. (2019), 'The "Inner Weakness": Merleau-Ponty on Intersubjectivity, Subjectivity, and Husserlian Phenomenology', in A. Falcato and L. Aguiar de Sousa (eds), *Phenomenological Approaches to Intersubjectivity and Values*, 49–82, Newcastle upon Tyne: Cambridge Scholars Publishing.

Allen, M., ed. (2017), 'Critical Incident Method', in *The SAGE Encyclopedia of Communication Research Methods*, Thousand Oaks, CA: SAGE.

American Psychological Association/APA (2017), *Ethical Principles of Psychologists and Code of Conduct*, Washington, DC: APA (accessed 21 June 2022).

Ammann, M. (2018), 'Leadership for Learning as Experience: Introducing the Use of Vignettes for Research on Leadership Experiences in Schools', *International Journal of Qualitative Methods*, 17 (1): 1–13.

Arendt, H. (1960), *Vita activa oder Vom tätigen Leben*, Stuttgart: Kohlhammer Verlag.

Arrighetti, G. (2007), 'Anekdote und Biographie', in M. Erler and S. Schorn (eds), *Die griechische Biographie in hellenistischer Zeit: Akten*

des internationalen Kongresses vom 26.-29. Juli 2006 in Würzburg,
79–100, Berlin: De Gruyter.

Bachelard, G. ([1988] 1990), *Fragments of a Poetics of Fire*, Dallas, TX:
Dallas Institute of Humanities and Culture.

Baron-Cohen, S. and J. E. Harrison, eds (1997), *Synaesthesia: Classic and
Contemporary Readings*, Cambridge, MA: Blackwell.

Barthel, C. (2010), 'Fallanalyse als Form forschenden Lernens', in
C. Barthel and C. Lorei (eds), *Empirische Forschungsmethoden:
Eine praxisorientierte Einführung für die Bachelor- und
Masterstudiengänge der Polizei*, 231–65, Frankfurt am Main: Verl. Für
Polizeiwissenschaft.

Beekman, T. (1987), 'Hand in Hand mit Sascha: Über Glühwürmchen,
Grandma Millie und einige andere Raumgeschichten. Im Anhang: Über
teilnehmende Erfahrung', in W. Lippitz and K. Meyer-Drawe (eds),
Kind und Welt: Phänomenologische Studien zur Pädagogik, 11–25,
Frankfurt am Main: Athenäum.

Blumenberg, H. (2006), *Beschreibung des Menschen*, ed. M. Sommer,
Frankfurt am Main: Suhrkamp.

Boon, W. (2021), 'Vignetten online schreiben', Universität Wein (accessed
11 February 2021).

Breithaupt, F. (2022), 'Robert Habeck ist der perfekte Erzähler', *Der
Spiegel* 24, 36–8, 11 June.

Brinkmann, M. (2011), 'Pädagogische Erfahrung – phänomenologische
und ethnographische Forschungsperspektiven', in I. M. Breinbauer and
G. Weiß (eds), *Orte des empirischen in der Bildungstheorie*, 60–80,
Würzburg: Königshausen & Neumann.

Brinkmann, M. (2012), *Pädagogische Übung: Praxis und Theorie einer
elementaren Lernform*, Paderborn: Ferdinand Schöningh.

Brinkmann, M. (2014), 'Verstehen, Auslegen und Beschreiben zwischen
Hermeneutik und Phänomenologie. Zum Verhältnis und zur Differenz
hermeneutischer Rekonstruktion und phänomenologischer Deskription
am Beispiel von Günther Bucks Hermeneutik der Erfahrung', in S.
Schenk and T. Pauls (eds), *Aus Erfahrung lernen: Anschlüsse an
Günther Buck*, 199–222, Paderborn: Ferdinand Schöningh.

Brinkmann, M. (2018, April 26), *Epoché: Einklammern, Anhalten,
Zurücktreten, um Anderes und Fremdes zu sehen. Zur Praxis der
phänomenologischen Epoché in der qualitativen Forschung*,
Conference Paper, Wittenberger Gespräche, Halle/Wittenberg.

Bromand, J. and G. Kreis, eds (2010), *Was sich nicht sagen lässt: Das
Nicht-Begriffliche in Wissenschaft, Kunst und Religion*, Berlin: Akademie.

Bruner, J. S. and D. R. Olson (1978), 'Symbole und Texte als Werkzeuge
des Denkens', in G. Steiner (ed.), *Die Psychologie des 20. Jahrhunderts:
Entwicklungspsychologie, Denkpsychologie, genetische Psychologie*,
306–21, München: Kindler.

Bube, A. (2022), 'To Abstract', in N. Vansieleghem and V. Mühleis (eds), *Artuarium – The Grammar of Art School*, 283, Ghent: Grafische Cel.

Buck, G. (1967), 'Kants Lehre vom Exempel', *Archiv für Begriffsgeschichte*, 11: 148–83.

Buck, G. (1981), *Hermeneutik und Bildung: Elemente einer verstehenden Bildungslehre*, München: Wilhelm Fink.

Buck, G. ([1967] 1989), *Lernen und Erfahrung – Epagogik: zum Begriff der didaktischen Induktion*, 3rd edn, Darmstadt: Wissenschaftliche Buchgesellschaft.

Busch, K. and I. Därmann, eds (2007), *Philosophie der Responsivität: Festschrift für Bernhard Waldenfels; Tagung aus Anlass des 70. Geburtstages von Bernhard Waldenfels am 11.6.–13.6.2004 an der Ruhr-Universität Bochum*, München: Wilhelm Fink.

Cannon, F. (2009), *Facets of Leadership: Turning Management Thinking into Management Practice*, Cirencester: Management Books 2000.

Churchill, S. D. (2012), 'Teaching Phenomenology by Way of "Second-Person Perspectivity" from My Thirty Years at the University of Dallas', *Indo-Pacific Journal of Phenomenology*, 12 (3): 1–14.

Clandinin, D. J. (2006), *Handbook of Narrative Inquiry*, Thousand Oaks, CA: SAGE.

Clandinin, D. J. (2019), *Journeys in Narrative Inquiry: The Selected Works of D. Jean Clandinin*, 1st edn, London: Routledge.

Cloos, P. (2010), 'Narrative Beobachtungsprotokolle: Konstruktion, Rekonstruktion und Verwendung', in F. Heinzl, W. Thole, P. Cloos and S. Köngeter (eds), *"Auf unsicherem Terrain": Ethnographische Forschung im Kontext des Bildungs- und Sozialwesens*, 181–91, Wiesbaden: VS Verlag für Sozialwissenschaften.

Connelly, F. M. and D. J. Clandinin (1990), 'Stories of Experience and Narrative Inquiry', *Educational Researcher*, 19 (5): 2–14.

Constant, D., S. Kiesler and L. Sproull (1994), 'What's Mine Is Ours, or Is It? A Study of Attitudes about Information Sharing', *Information Systems Research*, 5 (4): 400–21.

Dall'Alba, G. (2009), *Exploring Education through Phenomenology: Diverse Approaches*, Malden, MA: Wiley-Blackwell.

Denzin, N. K. and Y. S. Lincoln, eds (2011), *The SAGE Handbook of Qualitative Research*, Thousand Oaks, CA: SAGE.

Dewey, J. ([1925] 1995), *Erfahrung und Natur*, trans. M. Suhr, Frankfurt am Main: Suhrkamp.

Doman, G. (1990), *What to Do about Your Brain-Injured Child*, Philadelphia: The Better Baby Press.

Eco, U. (1988), *Wie man eine wissenschaftliche Abschlussarbeit schreibt*, Heidelberg: Quelle & Meyer.

Elliot, J. (2005), *Using Narrative in Social Research: Qualitative and Quantitative Approaches*, London: SAGE.

Eloff, I. (2021), 'Words of Wellbeing: Using Vignettes to Capture Meaningful Moments in an African Context', in V. Symeonidis and J. F. Schwarz (eds), *Erfahrungen verstehen – (Nicht-) Verstehen erfahren. Potential und Grenzen der Vignetten- und Anekdotenforschung in der Annäherung an das Phänomen Verstehen Erfahrungsorientierte Bildungsforschung*, Vol. 8, 117–26, Innsbruck: StudienVerlag.

Eloff, I., E. Agostini, A. Dittrich and K. Mathabathe (2023), 'Vignettes of Equality, Wellbeing and Teaching', in C. H. Mayer, E. Vanderheiden, O. Braun-Lewensohn, G. Chen, K. Sueda, B. Mangolothi, S. Safdar and S. Kim (eds), *Women's Empowerment for a Sustainable Future: Transcultural and Positive Psychology Perspectives*, 617–28, Cham: Springer.

Eloff, I., K. Mathabathe, E. Agostini and A.-K. Dittrich (2022), 'Teaching the Global Goals: Exploring the Experiences of Teacher Educators in an Online-Environment through Vignette Research', *Environmental Sciences Proceedings*, 15 (1): 5.

Erickson, F. (1986), 'Qualitative Methods in Research on Teaching', in M. C. Wittrock (ed.), *AERA Handbook of Research on Teaching*, 119–61, New York: Macmillan.

Fauser, P. (2016), 'Der Deutsche Schulpreis, seine Qualitätsbereiche und die einzelne Schule als Qualitätsagentur', in S.-I. Beutel, K. Höhmann, H. A. Pant and M. Schratz (eds), *Handbuch Gute Schule: Sechs Qualitätsbereiche für zukunftsweisende Praxis*, 170–81, Seelze: Kallmeyer.

Finch, J. (1987), 'The Vignette Technique in Survey Research', *Sociology*, 21 (1): 105–14.

Fink, E. (1976), *Nähe und Distanz: Phänomenologische Vorträge und Aufsätze*, ed. F.-A. Schwarz, München: Karl Alber.

Finlay, L. (2009), 'Debating Phenomenological Research', *Phenomenology & Practice*, 3 (1): 6–25.

Flick, U. ([1995] 2005), *Qualitative Sozialforschung: Eine Einführung*, ed. B. König, 3rd edn, Reinbek bei Hamburg: Rowohlt.

Foucault, M. ([1975] 1976), *Überwachen und Strafen: Die Geburt des Gefängnisses*, trans. W. Seitter, Frankfurt am Main: Suhrkamp.

Foucault, M. (1996), *Der Mensch ist ein Erfahrungstier – Gespräch mit Ducio Trombadori: Mit einem Vorwort von Wilhelm Schmid und einer Bibliographie von Andrea Hemminger*, Frankfurt am Main: Suhrkamp.

Frost, D. (2006), 'The Concept of "Agency" in Leadership for Learning', *Leading & Managing*, 12 (2): 19–28.

Fullan, M. (2019), *Nuance: Why Some Leaders Succeed and Others Fail*, Thousand Oaks: CA: Corwin.

Gabriel, G. (2010), 'Logische Präzision und ästhetische Prägnanz', in V. Kapp, K. Müller, K. Ridder, R. Wimmer and K. Zimmermann (eds), *Literaturwissenschaftliches Jahrbuch 51*, 375–90, Berlin: Duncker und Humblot.

Gadamer, H.-G. (1967), *Philosophie: Hermeneutik (Kleine Schriften)*, Tübingen: J. C. B. Mohn.

Gallagher, S. (2012), *Phenomenology*, Houndmills: Palgrave Macmillan.

Geelan, D. (2006), *Undead Theories: Constructivism, Eclecticism and Research in Education*, Rotterdam: Sense Publications.

Geertz, C. ([1973] 1991), *Dichte Beschreibung: Beiträge zum Verstehen kultureller Systeme*, Frankfurt am Main: Suhrkamp.

Giddens, A. (1984), *The Constitution of Society: Outline of the Theory of Structuration*, Cambridge: Polity Press.

Heinämaa, S. (2019), 'Epoché as a Personal Transformation: On the Similarities between the Philosophical Change of Attitude and Religious Conversions', *Phänomenologische Forschungen*, 2: 133–60.

Heldbjerg, G. and D. van Liempd (2018), 'Vignettes in Critical Theory Investigations', in P. V. Freytag and L. Young, *Collaborative Research Design: Working with Business for Meaningful Findings*, 313–40, Singapore: Springer.

Hirschauer, S. and K. Amann, eds (1997), *Die Befremdung der eigenen Kultur: Zur ethnographischen Herausforderung soziologischer Empirie*, Frankfurt am Main: Suhrkamp.

Hitzler, F. (2000), *Methoden der Kindheitsforschung: Ein Überblick über Forschungszugänge zur kindlichen Perspektive*, Weinheim: Juventa.

Holloway, I. and D. Freshwater (2007), 'Vulnerable Story Telling: Narrative Research in Nursing', *Journal of Research in Nursing*, 12 (6): 703–11.

Hughes, R. and M. Huby (2004), 'The Construction and Interpretation of Vignettes in Social Research', *Social Work and Social Sciences Review*, 11 (1): 36–51.

Humphreys, M. (2005), 'Getting Personal: Reflexivity and Autoethnographic Vignettes', *Qualitative Inquiry*, 11 (6): 840–60.

Husserl, E. (1962), *Die Krisis der europäischen Wissenschaften und die transzendentale Phänomenologie, Husserliana VI*, Den Haag: Martinus Nijhoff.

Husserl, E. (1973), *Cartesianische Meditationen und die Pariser Vorträge, Husserliana I*, Den Haag: Martinus Nijhoff.

Husserl, E. (1990), *Die phänomenologische Methode*, Stuttgart: Reclam.

Husserl, E. (2001), *Logical Investigations, Volume 1*, trans. J. N. Findlay, London: Routledge.

Husserl, E. (2002), *Zur phänomenologischen Reduktion: Texte aus dem Nachlass (1926–1935)*, 1st edn, Dordrecht: Springer.

Kant, I. (1797), 'Metaphysik der Sitten: Metaphysische Anfangsgründe der Tugendlehre II. Ethische Methodenlehre. Erster Abschnitt: Die ethische Didaktik', in M. Holzinger, *KAA VI*, 203–493, Berlin: Holzinger.

Kirmayer, L. J., C. M. Fletcher and L. J. Boothroyd (1997), 'Inuit Attitudes toward Deviant Behavior: A Vignette Study', *Journal of Nervous and Mental Disease*, 185 (2): 78–86.

Koller, H.-C. ([2011] 2018), *Bildung anders denken: Einführung in die Theorie transformatorischer Bildungsprozesse*, 2nd edn, Stuttgart: Kohlhammer.

Krenn, S. (2017), *Ergriffen sein im Lernprozess*, Bad Heilbrunn: Klinkhardt.

Küpers, W. M. (2015), *Phenomenology of the Embodied Organization: The Contribution of Merleau-Ponty for Organizational Studies and Practice*, Basingstoke: Palgrave Macmillan.

Labov, W. and J. Waletzky (1967), 'Narrative Analysis', in J. Helm (ed.), *Essays on the Verbal and Visual Arts*, 12–44, Seattle: University of Washington Press.

Laing, R. D. (1967), *The Politics of Experience*, New York: Pantheon Books.

Lamnek, S. ([1988] 2010), *Qualitative Sozialforschung: Lehrbuch*, 5th edn, Weinheim, Basel: Beltz.

Langer, M. M. (1989), *Merleau-Ponty's Phenomenology of Perception: A Guide and Commentary*, London: Macmillan Press.

Latour, B. (1997), Ein neuer Empirismus, ein neuer Realismus, Mittelweg 36: Zeitschrift des Hamburger Instituts für Sozialforschung, 6 (1): 40–52.

Lévinas, E. (1983), *Die Spur des Anderen*, Freiburg: Karl Alber.

Lévinas, E. ([1974] 1992), *Jenseits des Seins oder anders als sein geschieht*, trans. T. Wiemer, Freiburg: Karl Alber.

Lindow, I. (2013), *Literaturunterricht als Fall: Kasuistisches Wissen von Deutschlehrenden*, Wiesbaden: Springer-Verlag.

Lippitz, W. (1987), 'Phänomenologie als Methode? Zur Geschichte und Aktualität des phänomenologischen Denkens in der Pädagogik', in W. Lippitz and K. Meyer-Drawe (eds), *Kind und Welt: Phänomenologische Studien zur Pädagogik*, 101–30, Frankfurt am Main: Athenäum.

Lippitz, W. (2003), *Differenz und Fremdheit: Phänomenologische Studien in der Erziehungswissenschaft*, Frankfurt am Main: Suhrkamp.

Lipps, H. (1941), 'Das Schamgefühl', in Strassburger Wissenschaftliche Gesellschaft (eds), *Die menschliche Natur, Werke*, Vol. 3, 29–43, Frankfurt am Main: Vittorio Klostermann.

Lüders, C. (2000), 'Beobachten im Feld und Ethnographie', in U. Flick, E. v. Kardorff and I. Steinke (eds), *Qualitative Forschung: Ein Handbuch*, 384–401, Reinbek bei Hamburg: Rowohlt.

Matthiesen, U. (1985), *Das Dickicht der Lebenswelt und die Theorie des kommunikativen Handelns*, München: Wilhelm Fink.

McGregor, J. (2014), 'On Leadership: Remembering Leadership Sage Warren Bennis', *The Washington Post*, 4 August (accessed 30 July 2020).

McKerracher, A. (2019), *What It Means to Write: Creativity and Metaphor*, Montreal: McGill–Queen's University Press.

Merleau-Ponty, M. ([1948] 1964), *Sense and Nonsense*, trans. H. L. Dreyfus and P. A. Dreyfus, Evanston, IL: Northwestern University Press.

Merleau-Ponty, M. ([1942] 1976), *Die Struktur des Verhaltens*, ed. C. F.
Graumann and A. Métraux, trans. B. Waldenfels, Berlin: Walter de
Gruyter.

Merleau-Ponty, M. ([1945] 2009), *Phenomenology of Perception*, trans.
C. Smith, London: Routledge.

Meyer-Drawe, K. (1996), 'Vom anderen lernen: Phänomenologische
Betrachtungen in der Pädagogik. Schaller zum siebzigsten Geburtstag',
in M. Borrelli and J. Ruhloff (eds), *Deutsche Gegenwartspädagogik*,
Vol. 2, 85–99, Baltmannweiler: Schneider-Verlag Hohengehren.

Meyer-Drawe, K. (2000), *Illusionen von Autonomie: Diesseits von
Ohnmacht und Allmacht des Ich*, Mainz: Kirchheim.

Meyer-Drawe, K. ([1984] 2001), *Leiblichkeit und Sozialität:
Phänomenologische Beiträge zu einer pädagogischen Theorie der
Inter-Subjektivität*, 3rd edn, München· Wilhelm Fink.

Meyer-Drawe, K. (2003), 'Lernen als Erfahrung', *Zeitschrift für
Erziehungswissenschaft*, 6 (4): 505–14.

Meyer-Drawe, K. (2010), 'Zur Erfahrung des Lernens: Eine
phänomenologische Skizze', *Filosofija*, 18 (3): 6–17.

Meyer-Drawe, K. (2011a), 'Staunen – ein "sehr philosophisches Gefühl"',
Etica & Politica, 13 (1): 196–205.

Meyer-Drawe, K. (2011b), 'Empfänglichsein für die Welt: Ein Beitrag zur
Bildungstheorie', in A. Dörpinghaus and A. Nießeler (eds), *Dinge in
der Welt der Bildung: Bildung in der Welt der Dinge*, 13–28,
Würzburg: Königshausen & Neumann.

Meyer-Drawe, K. (2012a), 'Vorwort', in M. Schratz, J.-F. Schwarz and
T. Westfall-Greiter, *Lernen als bildende Erfahrung: Vignetten in der
Praxisforschung*, 11–15, Innsbruck: StudienVerlag.

Meyer-Drawe, K. ([2008] 2012b), *Diskurse des Lernens*, 2nd edn,
München: Wilhelm Fink.

Meyer-Drawe, K. (2013). 'Lernen braucht Lehren', in P. Fauser, W. Beutel
and J. John (eds), *Pädagogische Reform: Anspruch – Geschichte –
Aktualität*, 89–97, Jena: Klett Kallmeyer.

Meyer-Drawe, K. (2017), 'Phenomenology as a Philosophy of Experience
– Implications for Pedagogy', in M. Ammann, T. Westfall-Greiter and
M. Schratz (eds), *Erfahrungen deuten – Deutungen erfahren:
Vignettes and Anecdotes as Research, Evaluation and Mentoring Tool
Erfahrungsorientierte Bildungsforschung*, Vol. 3, 13–21, Innsbruck:
StudienVerlag.

Meyer-Drawe, K. (2020), 'Wahrnehmung als pädagogische Übung:
Theoretische und praxisorientierte Auslotungen einer phänomenologisch
orientierten Bildungsforschung', in H. K. Peterlini, I. Cennamo and
J. Donlic (eds), *Wahrnehmung als pädagogische Übung: Theoretische
und praxisorientierte Auslotungen einer phänomenologisch orientierten*

Bildungsforschung. Erfahrungsorientierte Bildungsforschung, Vol. 7, 13–24, Innsbruck: StudienVerlag.

Miles, M. (1990), 'New Methods for Qualitative Data Collection and Analysis: Vignettes and Prestructured Cases', *Qualitative Studies in Education*, 3 (1): 37–51.

Moran, D. (2008), 'The Phenomenological Approach: An Introduction', in L. Introna, F. Ilharco and É. Faÿ (eds), *Phenomenology, Organisation and Technology*, 21–41, Lisboa: Universidade Católica Editora.

Moran, D. (2015), 'Husserl on Human Subjects as Sense-Givers and Sense-Apprehenders in a World of Significance', *Discipline Filosofiche*, 25 (2): 9–34.

Müller, B. K. (1995), 'Das Allgemeine und das Besondere beim sozialpädagogischen und psychoanalytischen Fallverstehen', *Zeitschrift für Pädagogik*, 41 (5): 697–708.

Ollerenshaw, J. A. and J. W. Creswell (2002), 'Narrative Research: A Comparison of Two Restorying Data Analysis Approaches', *Qualitative Inquiry*, 8 (3): 329–47.

Peterlini, H. K. (2017), 'Die Geburt des Pathos: Performative Anstöße zu pädagogischen Verstehens- und Handlungsmöglichkeiten durch Vignetten, Zeichnungen und szenische Darbietung', in M. Schratz, M. Ammann and T. Westfall-Greiter (eds), *Erfahrungen deuten – Deutungen erfahren: Experiential Vignettes and Anecdotes as Research, Evaluation and Mentoring Tool. Erfahrungsorientierte Bildungsforschung*, Vol. 3, 41–60, Innsbruck: StudienVerlag.

Peterlini, H. K. (2019), 'Falsche Kinder in der richtigen Schule – oder umgekehrt? Auslotung eines Perspektivenwechsels von selektiven Normalitätsvorstellungen hin zu einer Phänomenologie des "So-Seins"', in J. Donlic, E. Jaksche-Hoffman and H. K. Peterlini (eds), *Ist inklusive Schule möglich? Nationale und internationale Perspektiven*, 41–60, Bielefeld: Transcript.

Peterlini, H. K. (2020), 'Der zweifältige Körper: Die Leib-Körper-Differenz als diskriminierungskritische Perspektive – Vignettenforschung zu Rassismus, Sexismus und Behinderung', in H. K. Peterlini, I. Cennamo and J. Donlic (eds), *Wahrnehmung als pädagogische Übung: Theoretische und praxisorientierte Auslotungen der phänomenologisch orientierten Bildungsforschung. Erfahrungsorientierte Bildungsforschung*, Vol. 7, 25–45, Innsbruck: StudienVerlag.

Piaget, J. and B. Inhelder (1969), *The Psychology of the Child*, New York: Basic Books.

Rathgeb, G., S. Krenn and M. Schratz (2017), 'Erfahrungen zum Ausdruck verhelfen', in M. Ammann, T. Westfall-Greiter and M. Schratz (eds), *Erfahrungen deuten – Deutungen erfahren: Experiential Vignettes and Anecdotes as Research, Evaluation and Mentoring Tool. Erfahrungsorientierte Bildungsforschung*, Vol. 3, 95–106, Innsbruck: StudienVerlag.

Rieger-Ladich, M. (2014), 'Erkenntnisquellen eigener Art? Literarische Texte als Stimulanzien erziehungswissenschaftlicher Reflexion', *Zeitschrift für Pädagogik*, 60 (3): 350–66.

Rinofner-Kreidl, S. (2009), 'Scham und Schuld: Zur Phänomenologie selbstbezüglicher Gefühle', *Phänomenologische Forschungen*, 1: 137–73.

Rosa, H. (2018), *Unverfügbarkeit*, Salzburg: Residenz Verlag.

Rosa, H. ([2016] 2019), *Resonanz: Eine Soziologie der Weltbeziehung*, Berlin: Suhrkamp.

Rumpf, H. (2010), *Was hätte Einstein gedacht, wenn er nicht Geige gespielt hätte? Gegen die Verkürzungen des etablierten Lernbegriffs*, Weinheim: Juventa.

Salkind, N. J., ed. (2010), *Encyclopedia of Research Design*, Thousand Oaks, CA: SAGE.

Sartre, J.-P. ([1943] 1980), *Das Sein und das Nichts: Versuch einer phänomenologischen Ontologie*, Reinbek bei Hamburg: Rowohlt.

Scharmer, C. O. (2007), *Theory U: Leading from the Future as It Emerges: The Social Technology of Presencing*, Cambridge, MA: Society for Organizational Learning.

Schleicher, A., (2018), *PISA 2018: Insights and Interpretations*, Paris: OECD.

Schley, W. and M. Schratz (2021), *Führen mit Präsenz und Empathie: Werkzeuge zur schöpferischen Neugestaltung von Schule und Unterricht*, Weinheim: Beltz.

Schratz, M. (1994), 'Wissen schaffen, Menschen bewegen: Ein Beitrag zur Alphabetisierung sinnlicher Erfahrungen', in H. Hierdeis and M. Schratz (eds), *Mit den Sinnen begreifen: 10 Anregungen zu einer erfahrungsorientierten Pädagogik*, 117–34, Innsbruck: StudienVerlag.

Schratz, M., M. Ammann, N. Anderegg, A. Bergmann, M. Gregorzewsky, W. Mauersberg and V. Möltner (2022), *Lernseits führen: Den Facettenreichtum im Schulleben erkunden*, Hannover: Kallmeyer.

Schratz, M., J. F. Schwarz and T. Westfall-Greiter (2012), *Lernen als bildende Erfahrung: Vignetten in der Praxisforschung Erfolgreich im Lehrberuf*, Vol. 8, Innsbruck: StudienVerlag.

Schratz, M., J. F. Schwarz and T. Westfall-Greiter (2013), 'Looking at Two Sides of the Same Coin: Phenomenologically Oriented Vignette Research and Its Implications for Teaching and Learning', *Studia Paedagogica*, 18 (4): 57–73.

Schratz, M. and R. Walker (1995), *Research as Social Change: New Opportunities for Qualitative Research*, London: Routledge.

Schuhmann, S. (2017), 'Das Potential von Fallanalysen (Kasuistik) für die Frühpädagogik', *Kita-Fachtexte* (accessed 19 September 2018).

Schulz, M. (2010), 'Gefrorene Momente des Geschehens', in F. Heinzl, W. Thole, P. Cloos, and S. Köngeter (eds), *"Auf unsicherem Terrain": Ethnographische Forschung im Kontext des Bildungs- und Sozialwesens*, 71–9, Wiesbaden: VS Verlag für Sozialwissenschaften.

Schwarz, J. F. (2012), 'Lernseits forschen: Eine Akzentuierung', *Erziehung & Unterricht*, 9–10: 888–92.

Schwarz, J. F. (2018), *Zuschreibung als wirkmächtiges Phänomen in der Schule*, Innsbruck: StudienVerlag.

Serrat, O. (2017), 'The Critical Incident Technique', in O. Serrat, *Knowledge Solutions*, 1077–83, Singapore: Springer.

Smith, D. W. (2018), 'Phenomenology', *The Stanford Encyclopedia of Philosophy*, Summer 2018 Edition (accessed 30 July 2021).

Sokolowski, R. (2000), *Introduction to Phenomenology*, Cambridge: Cambridge University Press.

Steiner, E. (2014), 'Kasuistik – ein Fall für angehende und praktizierende Lehrpersonen', *Beiträge zur Lehrerinnen- und Lehrerbildung*, 32 (1): 6–20.

Stieve, C. (2010), 'Sich von Kindern irritieren lassen: Chancen phänomenologischer Ansätze für eine Ethnographie der frühen Kindheit', in G. E. Schäfer and R. Staege (eds), *Frühkindliche Lernprozesse verstehen: Ethnographische und phänomenologische Beiträge zur Bildungsforschung*, 23–50, Weinheim und Basel: Juventa.

Swart, M. L. (2021), 'Understanding How Hope Manifests for South African Youth during Times of Adversity', Unpublished MA Diss., University of Pretoria.

Tanaka, S. (2015), 'Intercorporeality as a Theory of Social Cognition', *Theory & Psychology*, 25 (4): 455–72.

Van Manen, M. (1979), 'The Phenomenology of Pedagogic Observation', *Canadian Journal of Education*, 4 (1): 5–16.

Van Manen, M. (1986), *The Tone of Teaching*, Portsmouth, NH: Heinemann.

Van Manen, M. (1990), *Researching Lived Experience: Human Science for an Action Sensitive Pedagogy*, Albany, NY: New York Press.

Van Manen, M. (2016), *Phenomenology of Practice: Meaning-Giving Methods in Phenomenological Research and Writing*, New York: Routledge.

Van Manen, M. and M. Van Manen (2021), *Classic Writings for a Phenomenology of* Practice, New York: Routledge.

Viergever, R. F. (2019), 'The Critical Incident Technique: Method or Methodology?', *Qualitative Health Research*, 29 (7): 1065–79.

Vrasidas, C. (2001), 'Making the Familiar Strange – and Interesting – Again: Interpretivism and Symbolic Interactionism in Educational Technology Research', in W. Heinecke and J. Willis (eds), *Research Methods in Educational Technology*, 81–99, Greenwich, CT: Information Age Publishing.

Waldenfels, B. (1992), *Einführung in die Phänomenologie*, Weinheim und Basel: Beltz.

Waldenfels, B. (1994), *Antwortregister*, Frankfurt am Main: Suhrkamp.

Waldenfels, B. (1999), *Vielstimmigkeit der Rede*, Frankfurt am Main: Suhrkamp.

Waldenfels, B. (2000), *Das leibliche Selbst*, Frankfurt am Main: Suhrkamp.

Waldenfels, B. (2002), *Bruchlinien der Erfahrung: Phänomenologie, Psychoanalyse, Phänomenotechnik*, Frankfurt am Main: Suhrkamp.

Waldenfels, B. (2004a), 'Das Fremde im Eigenen: Der Ursprung der Gefühle', *Der Blaue Reiter*, 2: 27–31.

Waldenfels, B. (2004b), 'Phänomenologie zwischen Pathos und Response', in W. Hogrebe (ed.), *Grenzen und Grenzüberschreitungen*, 813–25, Berlin: Akademie.

Waldenfels, B. (2006), *Grundmotive einer Phänomenologie des Fremden*, Frankfurt am Main: Suhrkamp.

Waldenfels, B. (2007), 'An Stelle von', in K. Busch and I. Därmann (eds), *"Pathos": Konturen eines kulturwissenschaftlichen Grundbegriffs*, 33–50, Bielefeld: Transcript.

Waldenfels, B. ([1987] 2013a), *Ordnung im Zwielicht*, 2nd edn, Boston: BRILL.

Waldenfels, B. ([1998] 2013b), *Sinnesschwellen: Studien zur Phänomenologie des Fremden*, 3rd edn, Frankfurt am Main: Suhrkamp.

Wensierski, H.-J. (2006), 'Pädagogische Kasuistik', in H.-H. Krüger and C. Grunert (eds), *Wörterbuch Erziehungswissenschaft*, 259–64, Leverkusen-Opladen: Barbara Budrich.

Wernet, A. (2006), *Hermeneutik – Kasuistik – Fallverstehen. Eine Einführung*, Stuttgart: W. Kohlhammer Verlag.

Westfall-Greiter, T. and H. Dienhofer (2017), 'From Evidence-Based to Evidence Generating Practice: Implications for Education Research in the Context of Innovation', in M. Ammann, T. Westfall-Greiter and M. Schratz (eds), *Erfahrungen deuten – Deutungen erfahren: Vignettes and Anecdotes as Research, Evaluation and Mentoring Tool*, 77–94, Innsbruck: StudienVerlag.

Whittemore, R., S. K. Chase and C. L. Mandle (2001), 'Validity in Qualitative Research', *Qualitative Health Research*, 11 (4): 522–37.

Zahavi, D. (2019), *Phenomenology: The Basics*, London: Routledge.

INDEX